Work
Reimagined

The AI Era

By
Rafael Navarro

Work Reimagined

The AI Era

Table of Contents

Introduction 1

Chapter 1: The AI Revolution 4
    Understanding Artificial Intelligence 4
    The History and Evolution of AI 7

Chapter 2: The Role of AI in the Workplace 11
    AI Integration in Different Industries 11
    Impact on Job Roles and Responsibilities 15

Chapter 3: Emerging AI Technologies 19
    Machine Learning and Deep Learning 19
    Natural Language Processing Applications 22

Chapter 4: Redefining Human-Machine Collaboration 26
    Synergy Between Humans and AI 27
    Advantages of Human-AI Partnerships 30

Chapter 5: The Future of Work 34
    Predictions and Trends in the AI Era 34
    What Jobs Will Thrive 38

Chapter 6: Reshaping Skillsets for an AI-Driven World 41
    Skills in Demand in the AI Era 41
    Lifelong Learning and Adaptability 44

Chapter 7: Overcoming Challenges in AI Implementation ... 48
    Addressing Ethical Concerns 48
    Mitigating Bias in AI Systems 51

Chapter 8: Strategies for Businesses in the AI Age 55
Embracing Digital Transformation 55
Innovating Business Models with AI 58

Chapter 9: AI in Decision-Making.. 61
Enhancing Business Strategies 62
Data-Driven Decision Processes.. 64

Chapter 10: The Impact of AI on Organizational Culture................. 68
Building an AI-Friendly Workplace Environment......................... 68
Fostering a Culture of Innovation 71

Chapter 11: Leadership in the AI Era.. 74
Developing AI-Ready Leaders.. 74
Navigating Change and Uncertainty 77

Chapter 12: AI and the Global Economy 81
Economic Implications of AI... 81
International Collaboration in AI Advancements....................... 84

Chapter 13: Ensuring a Human-Centric AI Future............................ 88
Prioritizing Human Values.. 88
Safeguarding Human Rights 92

Chapter 14: Legal and Regulatory Considerations 95
Navigating AI Legislation.. 95
Ensuring Compliance and Transparency 99

Chapter 15: AI-Driven Customer Experience.................................... 102
Personalization and Customer Insights 102
Building Customer Trust with AI 106

Chapter 16: Automating Routine Tasks 109
Efficiency Through Automation 109
Balancing Automation and Human Input....................................... 112

Chapter 17: AI in Talent Acquisition and Management................... 116
AI Tools for Recruitment 116

Employee Development with AI Support......................................119

Chapter 18: The Role of AI in Corporate Social Responsibility......123
Leveraging AI for Social Good...123
Aligning AI Initiatives with CSR Goals 126

Chapter 19: AI-Enhanced Remote Work 130
Tools and Technologies for Virtual Collaboration....................130
Challenges and Opportunities in Remote Work........................133

Chapter 20: Data Privacy and Security in the AI Era 137
Protecting Sensitive Information 137
AI Threats and Countermeasures 141

Chapter 21: AI in Supply Chain and Logistics..........................144
Optimizing Supply Chain Operations...................................144
AI-Driven Inventory Management 147

Chapter 22: Harnessing AI for Innovation................................151
Accelerating Research and Development 151
Unlocking Creative Potential with AI 154

Chapter 23: Measuring AI's Impact on Business Performance 158
Metrics and Analytics for AI Assessment 158
Benchmarking AI-Enabled Success.......................................161

Chapter 24: Preparing for the Unknown.................................165
Anticipating Future Developments in AI................................165
Building Resilience in a Changing Landscape.........................168

Chapter 25: Collaborative AI: A New Era of Innovation.............172
Case Studies of Successful AI Collaboration.............................173
Lessons Learned from AI Integration 176

Conclusion 180

Appendix A: Resources for Further Learning 182

Introduction

As we stand on the edge of a new frontier, the impact of artificial intelligence (AI) reverberates through every corner of the modern workplace. The dramatic emergence of AI technologies is not just a momentary blip on the radar of technological advancement but a transformative force reshaping how we approach our work, our industries, and even our understanding of human potential. We've seen revolutions in the past, like the industrial age and the digital revolution, but the AI revolution promises to intersect every aspect of business and personal life in ways we are only beginning to understand.

AI is no longer confined to the realms of science fiction. It has become an integral part of our daily lives, assisting us from optimizing logistics and supply chains to providing recommendations on streaming platforms. The transition from a human-only ecosystem to one where machines play an active partnership role is happening faster than most anticipated. It's a shift that requires not only technological but also cultural adaptation, demanding new strategies to harness AI's potential while addressing the ethical and practical implications it presents.

As businesses grapple with integrating AI technologies, leaders face the dual challenge of navigating rapid technological changes while ensuring their workforce remains engaged and empowered. AI offers the promise of enhanced productivity, efficiency, and innovation, but it also raises questions about job displacement and the evolving nature of work itself. For business leaders, striking that balance between technological advancement and human-centric approaches is paramount.

Understanding AI's role in this new landscape demands more than passive acceptance. It necessitates active participation from individuals willing to engage with the technology shaping their fields. Whether you're a seasoned executive steering your company through change or a tech enthusiast keen on the latest advancements, AI's trajectory provides fertile ground for exploration and adaptation. It's not merely about survival; it's about identifying opportunities that AI presents and leveraging them to create a competitive edge.

This book serves as a guide, a beacon for those navigating this evolving terrain. Through insights and strategies, it aims to equip readers with the tools necessary to not just cope but thrive in an AI-driven environment. By exploring the various dimensions of AI—from machine learning and natural language processing to the impact on job roles and organizational culture—readers will gain a comprehensive view of what it means to work alongside intelligent systems.

At the heart of the AI conversation is a deep inquiry into the human-machine relationship. How do we foster a synergy that enriches workplace dynamics? As AI systems take on more tasks, humans are liberated to focus on creativity, critical thinking, and complex problem-solving. This partnership, if managed correctly, can lead to a workplace where the efficiency of machines and the ingenuity of humans operate in concert, each enhancing the other.

However, as we delve deeper into AI's capabilities, ethical considerations come to the forefront. How do we ensure fairness, transparency, and accountability in AI systems? These questions are crucial as businesses adopt AI-driven decision processes, influencing everything from recruitment to customer interaction. Advocating for human-centric AI necessitates a commitment to safeguarding human values and rights in an increasingly automated world.

Preparing for an AI-rich future also involves embracing adaptability and a mindset of lifelong learning. As AI reshapes the skills in demand, those who are agile and open to continuous education will find themselves at an advantage. The workplace of tomorrow requires individuals who are not just technically proficient but also adept at navigating the complex interplay of human and machine capabilities.

Moreover, AI's implications extend beyond individual businesses to global economic landscapes, influencing everything from international collaboration to competitiveness on the world stage. By understanding these broader economic ramifications, business leaders can position themselves and their organizations strategically in the global marketplace.

It's not all challenges and changes, though. The AI revolution holds the promise of tremendous social good. From improving healthcare outcomes to enhancing environmental sustainability, AI offers tools to address some of the most pressing issues of our time. When aligned with corporate social responsibility goals, AI can become a powerful ally in building a better world.

This introduction sets the stage for a journey into the intricate tapestry of AI's role in the workplace and beyond. It's an invitation to explore how AI can be harnessed to unlock new levels of productivity, innovation, and collaboration. As you embark on this exploration, keep in mind that the goal is not just to understand but to actively shape the future where humans and AI work hand-in-hand.

Chapter 1:
The AI Revolution

As we stand on the cusp of an AI revolution, it's clear that artificial intelligence is no longer a distant notion of the future but an essential reality reshaping the foundation of our workplaces and societies. This transformation echoes through the hallways of various industries, shaking up traditional roles and responsibilities while promising unprecedented efficiency and innovation. Understanding the catalysts of this revolution begins with demystifying AI itself—seeing past the buzzwords to grasp its nuances. Although AI's inception dates back decades, its evolution has accelerated remarkably in recent years, fueled by breakthroughs in data processing and computing power. This chapter explores this seismic shift, urging professionals and leaders to harness AI's potential not just to survive but to thrive in a world that's rapidly changing. With a world increasingly defined by algorithms, the ability to adapt and adopt transformative strategies becomes not just advisable, but indispensable for success in the modern age. The digital frontier promises challenges and opportunities alike, offering those willing to evolve a pivotal role in crafting the future we all share.

Understanding Artificial Intelligence

At the heart of the AI revolution lies a fundamental shift in how we define and engage with intelligence. In the simplest terms, artificial intelligence can be understood as the development of computer systems that can perform tasks typically requiring human intelligence. These tasks include visual perception, speech recognition, decision-making, and language translation. Yet, the scope of AI is vastly more intricate, echoing the diverse ways in which it can be embedded into the fabric of modern life and work.

AI is not a singular technology but a grand tapestry of tools and techniques. It encompasses machine learning, natural language processing, computer vision, and robotics—all woven together under the notion of creating systems that can learn and adapt. Machine learning, a core subset of AI, is particularly instrumental, allowing systems to improve their performance over time without being explicitly programmed for every task. We can think of it as the engine driving most AI innovations today.

Perhaps one of the most compelling aspects of AI is its ability to learn from data. In the information-rich world we inhabit, data is abundant. AI's capability to process and draw insights from massive datasets is unmatched, providing organizations with a profound new tool for decision-making. Companies leverage AI-driven analytics to uncover patterns, predict trends, and even anticipate consumer behavior. The implications of this are wide-ranging: businesses can optimize operations, enhance customer experiences, and innovate in ways previously imagined only in science fiction.

Understanding AI also requires acknowledging its limitations. Despite its impressive capabilities, AI lacks the nuanced understanding and empathy inherent in human cognition. It's deterministic, bound by the parameters and data it is fed. These limitations emphasize the importance of discerning the appropriate contexts for AI application, an understanding that will define successful adoption in professional environments.

Diving deeper into AI's realm, we encounter the different forms it adopts. Narrow AI, or weak AI, is designed and trained for a specific task, such as facial recognition or voice assistants. It's the most common form present in our everyday lives and workplaces. On the horizon, however, is the elusive goal of developing general AI, which would be able to understand and learn any intellectual task that a human being can. This level of AI remains a subject of active research and ethical discourse, poised to redefine the nature of work and creativity itself if realized.

The transformative power of AI stems from its ability to autonomously execute tasks that, until now, required human intelligence and effort. This capability is fueled by the ceaseless march of computing power and data availability, offering a glimpse into a future where machines extend human capabilities in unprecedented ways. The AI revolution invites businesses to rethink traditional models, offering pathways to innovation, efficiency, and competitiveness in an increasingly automated world.

In professional settings, AI is not just an abstract concept but a practical asset shaping industry landscapes. It's instrumental in sectors such as healthcare, finance, and manufacturing—where it aids in diagnosing patients, assessing financial risks, and streamlining production processes, respectively. In each case, AI's applications are both diverse and deeply integrated, offering new routes for problem-solving and operational excellence.

Adopting AI, however, requires balance and foresight. Businesses must align technology integration with human values and ethical considerations, ensuring that AI supports, rather than supplants, the human workforce. The dialogue surrounding AI ethics, bias, and transparency is not just academic but a business imperative, guiding how organizations structure their AI strategies.

Moreover, AI's evolution compels us to redefine the skills required in modern workplaces. As AI systems take over routine tasks, human roles are poised to shift towards more strategic and creative functions.

This evolution underscores the necessity of lifelong learning and adaptability in the workforce—a theme that echoes throughout AI's ongoing narrative.

To perceive AI's true potential, we must look beyond its technological underpinnings and consider its societal impact. AI technologies have the potential to address global challenges, from climate change to healthcare access, suggesting a future where innovation serves the greater good. However, realizing this vision depends on inclusive collaboration across disciplines, industries, and governments.

As we navigate the AI revolution, understanding artificial intelligence isn't just about comprehending its mechanics but also about recognizing its potential to reshape our world. This understanding calls for a nuanced approach—one that appreciates both the opportunities AI presents and the responsibilities it entails. As business leaders and tech enthusiasts, embracing AI means not only adapting to change but actively participating in the creation of a future where technology and humanity evolve hand in hand.

The History and Evolution of AI

The journey of artificial intelligence (AI) is a tale marked by remarkable milestones and revolutionary ideas. This journey didn't begin in the 21st century; it has its roots deeply embedded in the philosophical and scientific pursuits of early thinkers who dared to dream of machines that could mimic human thought. As we delve into the history of AI, we see a series of evolutionary leaps, each propelled by breakthroughs in technology, spurred by human ingenuity.

To truly appreciate where AI stands today, it's essential to trace its origins back to ancient history. The concept of intelligent automatons dates as far back as Greek mythology, with stories of Hephaestus crafting servant machines and mechanical creatures. These myths, although not technological, laid the groundwork for human imagination about the potential of creating life-like machines.

Fast forward to the mid-20th century, and we encounter the profound influence of British mathematician and logician Alan Turing. In 1950, Turing introduced the idea of a machine's ability to exhibit intelligent behavior indistinguishable from that of a human in his seminal paper "Computing Machinery and Intelligence." This was the birth of the "Turing Test," a criterion that continues to inspire AI research today. Turing's vision ignited an intellectual firestorm, challenging the boundaries of what machines could achieve.

As we step into the late 1950s and early 1960s, we see the formal beginnings of AI as a scientific discipline. The Dartmouth Conference of 1956 is often cited as the birthplace of AI as an academic field. During this historic gathering, prominent scholars like John McCarthy, Marvin Minsky, and others proposed the development of machines capable of simulating every aspect of learning and intelligence. This era marked a period of optimistic predictions and ambitious projects.

During the 1960s and 70s, AI research witnessed significant advances in symbolic reasoning, a subfield focused on crafting algorithms that could manipulate symbols and solve problems logically. Programs like ELIZA, an early natural language processing endeavor, astonished the world by mimicking human conversation. Despite these achievements, AI faced its first "winter" in the 1970s, as expectations outpaced actual technological capabilities. Funding dried up, and skepticism set in, casting doubt over the field's promises.

Recovery arrived in the 1980s, with the resurgence of AI powered by expert systems. These systems, designed to emulate decision-making ability, found commercial success, especially in sectors like finance and medicine. The Japanese Fifth Generation Computer Systems project further revitalized interest, injecting enthusiasm and investment into

AI research globally. This period laid crucial groundwork for the next wave of AI innovations, even as another "winter" loomed in the late 1980s and early 1990s due to unmet grandiose predictions.

The dawn of the 21st century heralded a renaissance for AI, fueled primarily by the explosion of data and advancements in computational power. The proliferation of digital data ushered in a new age wherein machine learning and neural networks, long conceptualized, found fertile ground to flourish. Researchers began developing algorithms capable of learning from vast datasets, culminating in breakthroughs that transcended traditional boundaries.

Among these breakthroughs was the development of deep learning, a subset of machine learning inspired by the neural networks of the human brain. In 2012, a pivotal moment occurred when a neural network, AlexNet, achieved unprecedented accuracy in image recognition tasks, igniting a surge in AI research and applications. The subsequent decade saw AI achieving feats once deemed science fiction: self-driving cars, virtual assistants, and even creative endeavors such as art and music generation.

AI's evolution isn't just a tale of technological advancements; it's also a narrative intertwined with societal and ethical considerations. As AI systems have grown more capable, they've sparked debates about autonomy, accountability, and transparency. These discussions underscore the importance of ensuring that AI's evolution aligns with human values, championing innovation that uplifts rather than undermines our social fabric.

Today, as AI permeates both mundane and complex aspects of our lives, we stand at a crossroad of opportunities and challenges. The evolution of AI is far from complete; it's an ongoing journey shaping not just industries but the very essence of work and life. With AI's capabilities rapidly expanding, we find ourselves in a landscape where machines aren't merely tools but collaborators in redefining the future.

The history of AI serves as a testament to human curiosity and perseverance. We've witnessed an extraordinary transformation of AI from a concept discussed in academic circles to a powerhouse driving innovation across the globe. As we navigate the AI revolution, understanding this historical evolution empowers us with the perspectives needed to harness AI's potential responsibly and ethically, cementing its role as a catalyst for progress in the modern workplace.

Chapter 2:
The Role of AI in the Workplace

In the modern workplace, AI is rapidly becoming a catalyst for transformation, reshaping how businesses operate and how roles are defined. It's not just about efficiency but also about innovation, as AI allows companies to rethink traditional business models and processes. Organizations across various sectors are finding that integrating AI leads to smarter decision-making and greater agility. With AI systems taking on repetitive tasks, professionals can now focus on strategic and creative aspects of their jobs. This shift is paving the way for enhanced job satisfaction and productivity, as employees are empowered to leverage technology in new ways. As industries continue to embrace these changes, the collaboration between humans and machines is evolving into a powerful partnership that drives organizational success and fosters a culture of continuous improvement.

AI Integration in Different Industries

In the transforming landscape of modern business, AI's integration into various industries marks a profound shift in how organizations operate, innovate, and compete. From healthcare to finance and retail, AI's reach is vast and growing, poised to redefine industry standards and create new benchmarks for efficiency and effectiveness. As AI technologies mature, their applications become more refined, offering industries novel ways to surmount old challenges and embrace new opportunities.

In healthcare, AI stands as a pivotal tool for advancement. The industry leverages powerful algorithms to enhance diagnostics, personalize treatment plans, and manage patient data with unprecedented accuracy. For example, AI-powered imaging tools can detect anomalies in medical scans faster than human experts, reducing diagnostic errors and saving lives. Furthermore, AI supports the development of personalized medicine by analyzing vast genomic data, aiding in the crafting of treatment strategies tailored to individual patients. By automating routine administrative tasks, AI also liberates healthcare professionals to focus on patient care, thus enhancing the overall quality of service. As these technologies become more ingrained in healthcare settings, the potential for improved outcomes and operational efficiencies expands significantly.

The financial sector, with its mountains of data and need for precision, is another industry where AI is making significant inroads. Financial institutions are integrating AI to automate risk assessments, detect fraudulent activities, and optimize trading decisions. Machine learning algorithms analyze customer data to offer personalized financial advice and services, improving customer satisfaction and retention. Robo-advisors have emerged as a new frontier in this field, democratizing access to financial planning by offering affordable and efficient advisory services to a broader audience. This technological shift not only enhances the performance of financial institutions but also increases accessibility and transparency for consumers.

Retail, a dynamic and consumer-driven industry, leverages AI to enhance the customer experience and streamline operations. Through predictive analytics, retailers anticipate consumer trends, manage inventory efficiently, and tailor marketing strategies to individual preferences. AI-driven recommendation systems, such as those used by e-commerce giants, have revolutionized the shopping experience by offering personalized product suggestions that cater to consumer tastes and preferences. Additionally, AI facilitates automation in supply chain management, ensuring timely delivery and reducing operational costs. The integration of AI into retail thus enables businesses to provide a seamless shopping experience while optimizing their logistical frameworks.

Manufacturing is witnessing a transformation akin to an industrial revolution, powered by AI and the proliferation of smart technologies. AI-enhanced automation systems and robotics streamline production processes, optimize supply chains, and minimize waste. Predictive maintenance systems utilizing AI analyze data from machinery to foresee potential malfunctions and schedule timely interventions, reducing downtime significantly. Moreover, AI contributes to the innovation of product designs by simulating real-world usage scenarios, allowing for the creation of better products faster. This confluence of AI and manufacturing promises not only to boost productivity but also to foster a culture of continuous improvement and innovation.

In the energy sector, AI's potential is being harnessed to optimize resource management and promote sustainability. AI systems analyze energy consumption patterns to improve grid management, potentially reducing energy waste and costs. Smart grids powered by AI ensure a more efficient distribution of electricity, especially during peak times, thereby enhancing grid stability. Renewable energy management benefits significantly from AI, where predictive analytics assist in balancing supply and demand, ensuring a steady flow of energy from sources like wind and solar power. As environmental concerns mount globally, AI's capabilities in optimizing energy usage and integrating renewable sources become increasingly vital to achieving sustainability goals.

The transportation industry is evolving rapidly due to AI integration, with the advent of self-driving technologies leading the charge. Autonomous vehicles, once a concept of science fiction, are now a burgeoning reality, promising enhanced safety and efficiency in passenger and freight transportation. AI-driven logistics solutions optimize routes and manage traffic patterns, reducing fuel consumption and carbon footprints. Moreover, AI-powered customer service solutions in the transport industry, such as virtual assistants and chatbots, offer 24/7 support, improving customer interactions and service efficiency. The benefits of AI in transportation include safer roads, optimized operations, and a move towards environmentally friendly mobility solutions.

Agriculture, an industry foundational to human survival, is experiencing a renaissance with AI's integration. AI-powered data analytics and predictive modeling enhance yield by providing farmers with insights on crop health, pest infestations, and weather conditions. Smart farming technologies and drones equipped with AI systems facilitate precision agriculture, optimizing irrigation and fertilization tactics to maximize output while conserving resources. Furthermore, AI streamlines supply chain operations by forecasting demand and reducing waste through improved inventory management. By boosting productivity and sustainability, AI is helping farmers meet the growing global demand for food.

Education, an industry that molds future generations, is also seeing transformative changes with AI's emergence. AI systems are personalizing learning experiences, adapting educational content to suit individual learning paces and styles. Intelligent tutoring systems offer students immediate feedback and customized lessons, ensuring a better understanding of complex subjects. AI also aids in assessing educational performance, providing educators with insights into learning progress and areas requiring additional focus. This transformation ensures that education is inclusive, equitable, and oriented towards equipping learners with the skills necessary for a future driven by technological advancements.

Media and entertainment industries are exploring AI to create content and engage audiences in novel ways. AI algorithms curate and recommend content based on viewer preferences, creating a personalized viewing experience that keeps audiences engaged. Content creation is also receiving a boost from AI, with deep learning techniques generating realistic visuals and sound, creating immersive experiences in gaming and virtual reality. Furthermore, AI assists in streamlining production processes, reducing costs, and reaching larger audiences through targeted advertising. By harnessing AI, media and entertainment industries are engaging audiences more effectively and paving the way for innovative content exploration.

In each industry, the integration of AI leads to operational excellence, enhanced customer experiences, and a competitive edge in the marketplace. As these technologies continue to evolve and mature, their influence will extend further, reshaping the very fabric of industry as we know it. Businesses that embrace AI intelligently and strategically will not only thrive but also lead the charge towards a future defined by innovation and efficiency. This era of AI integration offers a canvas of possibilities, where industries reimagine their potential and redouble their impact on society, driving progress in an increasingly interconnected world.

Impact on Job Roles and Responsibilities

Artificial intelligence is reshaping the landscape of job roles and responsibilities at an unprecedented pace. As AI technologies continue to advance, they are not only automating routine tasks but also augmenting human capabilities in surprising ways. In the workplace, this dual nature of AI—automation and augmentation—brings both opportunities and challenges that are redefining what it means to work.

One of the most immediate impacts of AI on job roles is the shift of routine and repetitive tasks from human to machine. Tasks such as data entry, scheduling, and transaction processing are increasingly being performed by AI systems that can operate more efficiently and with fewer errors. While this shift might seem threatening to some job categories, especially those heavily reliant on manual and repetitive work, it also liberates employees from mundane tasks, allowing them to focus on more complex and creative endeavors.

With AI handling the monotony, employees are encouraged to develop skills that machines currently lack—such as emotional intelligence, complex problem-solving, and innovative thinking. As a result, the value of soft skills is increasing across various industries. The ability to communicate effectively, think critically, and lead with empathy is becoming even more essential. This shift requires not only retraining but also a change in mindset, where employees view their collaboration with AI as a partnership rather than competition.

The introduction of AI into workplaces also brings about significant changes in management strategies. Managers must now consider how AI tools can be leveraged to improve productivity and enhance the decision-making processes. This involves understanding the capabilities and limitations of AI systems and determining the best ways to integrate them alongside human employees. In doing so, it requires a redefinition of team dynamics, where both human and machine play complementary roles.

This shift towards a more AI-driven workplace prompts a re-evaluation of traditional job roles. New roles are emerging at the intersection of technology and domain expertise. Positions such as AI trainers, data analysts, and AI ethicists are becoming more common, emphasizing the need for interdisciplinary knowledge. These roles not only provide opportunities for career growth but also require a workforce that is adaptable and willing to engage in lifelong learning.

Moreover, the integration of AI isn't uniform across all sectors. Industries such as healthcare, finance, and manufacturing have seen more substantial AI adoption, leading to more pronounced changes in job roles. For instance, in healthcare, AI assists in diagnostics and treatment planning, which shifts the focus of medical professionals towards patient care and personalized medicine. In finance, algorithms perform real-time data analysis, altering the responsibilities of financial analysts to focus more on strategy and client consulting.

While AI brings about efficiency and innovation, it also necessitates a rethinking of areas such as ethics and accountability in the workplace. Decisions made by AI systems, particularly those impacting job roles, need to be scrutinized for bias and fairness. The responsibility to monitor these systems often falls on human employees, who must ensure that AI-enhanced processes align with organizational values and regulatory standards.

Furthermore, the evolving landscape of job roles and responsibilities requires organizations to invest in training and upskilling programs. Preparing employees for new roles involves not only technical education but also fostering a culture of continuous improvement and adaptability. Companies that prioritize workforce development are more likely to thrive in an AI-driven world, as they harness the full potential of their talent pool.

The transformation brought about by AI in job roles and responsibilities also poses questions about the future of employment. As certain roles become obsolete, the creation of new positions could potentially fill these gaps. However, this transition isn't always seamless, and there may be periods of adjustment where the demand for specific skills outpaces supply. Policymakers and business leaders must collaborate to address these challenges and ensure that the workforce remains robust and competitive.

Ultimately, AI is steering the workforce towards a future where job roles are more flexible and dynamic. The blend of machine efficiency and human creativity could lead to a more fulfilling work environment. For business leaders, the challenge lies in managing this transition effectively—capitalizing on AI's potential while ensuring that their people remain at the forefront of their organizational strategy.

As we navigate these changes, it's crucial for individuals to embrace lifelong learning and for organizations to build environments that foster innovation and collaboration. By doing so, we can harness AI's transformative power to redesign job roles and responsibilities that empower employees, drive economic growth, and enhance societal well-being.

Chapter 3:
Emerging AI Technologies

As we delve into the realm of emerging AI technologies, we stand on a precipice where innovation meets unprecedented opportunity. At this juncture, Machine Learning and Natural Language Processing serve as formidable pillars driving forward this technological renaissance. These groundbreaking advances unleash transformative potential across industries, underpinning powerful predictive analytics, and enhancing human-computer interactions in ways once confined to the realm of science fiction. By embracing these cutting-edge tools, businesses find themselves empowered to boost efficiency, create personalized customer experiences, and unlock creative solutions to complex problems. Yet with these advancements comes the responsibility to harness them wisely and ethically, ensuring that the symbiosis between humans and machines breeds a future where technology augments our capabilities, rather than overshadowing them. This intricate dance with AI beckons leaders, innovators, and enthusiasts alike to pivot, adapt, and lead with vision and foresight, laying the groundwork for a prosperous and AI-augmented future.

Machine Learning and Deep Learning

In the ever-expanding universe of artificial intelligence, machine learning and deep learning have emerged as two of the most significant forces shaping the landscape. With their ability to transform raw data into actionable insights, these technologies serve as the backbone for a multitude of AI applications driving change across industries. For business leaders and tech enthusiasts alike, understanding the nuances of these technologies is key to adapting and thriving in an AI-driven world.

Machine learning revolves around the concept of teaching computers to learn from data without being explicitly programmed. It's about finding patterns, predicting outcomes, and continuously improving performance through experience. Unlike traditional programming, where instructions are hardcoded, machine learning models adapt, refine, and evolve with every data point they process. This adaptability is what makes machine learning a cornerstone of modern AI technologies.

On a deeper level, we encounter deep learning—a subfield of machine learning that pushes the boundaries even further. Leveraging artificial neural networks modeled loosely after the human brain, deep learning dives into layers and layers of data to extract higher-level features and patterns. It's no wonder that deep learning powers so many innovations, from voice-activated assistance and image recognition to autonomous vehicles navigating complex environments.

Both machine learning and deep learning are reshaping industries by enhancing capabilities and redefining what's possible. In healthcare, for instance, these technologies are accelerating diagnostics with unprecedented accuracy. Algorithms can sift through vast amounts of medical images to detect anomalies that might escape the human eye. Such advancements not only optimize workflow but also have the potential to save lives by enabling early diagnosis and intervention.

Finance is an area where machine learning has taken firm root, automating trading systems, improving fraud detection, and personalizing customer experiences. The ability to analyze large datasets in real-time allows for more informed decision-making, minimizing risks, and maximizing returns. These technologies predict market trends, detect irregularities, and respond to queries with swiftness and efficiency.

In retail, personalization has reached new heights as companies harness the power of machine learning algorithms to dissect consumer habits and preferences. Recommender systems, such as those used by e-commerce giants, use past behavior to suggest products that customers are most likely to purchase. This not only enhances user experience but also drives sales by aligning inventory with customer demand more effectively.

While many industries are leveraging these technologies, the journey is not without its challenges. Developing robust, scalable machine learning models requires copious amounts of data and computational power. Not all organizations possess the resources to achieve this. Moreover, as these systems grow more complex, the risk of bias and error escalates, necessitating vigorous oversight and ethical considerations.

Business leaders must grapple with these challenges proactively. They need to build teams that are not only proficient technically but also aware of the societal impacts of their work. Creating transparent systems that stakeholders trust is paramount. Machine learning and deep learning are no longer isolated technical pursuits; they are intertwined with business strategy and cultural ethos.

The skills required in the era of machine learning are also evolving. Data scientists, machine learning engineers, and AI ethicists are among the roles that have rapidly risen in demand. Professionals need to be adept not only at crafting algorithms but also at communicating insights derived from complex data analyses to non-technical stakeholders.

Despite the hurdles, the promise of machine learning and deep learning is tantalizing. These technologies offer pathways to innovation that were once the stuff of science fiction. For businesses, the incentives to adopt and adapt are significant—those who can leverage these technologies effectively stand to gain a competitive edge.

One might wonder about the trajectory of these emerging technologies. Can machine learning and deep learning continue to evolve at the current pace? The answer is an optimistic one. With continual research and the advent of quantum computing on the horizon, the capabilities of these algorithms will likely continue to expand, reaching new frontiers previously deemed unattainable.

To integrate these technologies successfully, a strategic approach is essential. Organizations need to not only invest in technology but also foster a culture of learning and innovation. By doing so, they can empower employees at all levels to engage with AI technologies confidently and creatively.

In conclusion, machine learning and deep learning represent powerful instruments in the ongoing evolution of AI. For those poised to navigate this transformative era, the benefits are immense. With a blend of technical acumen, ethical foresight, and strategic innovation, entities can unlock these technologies' full potential and craft an exciting future in the AI landscape. As they say, the future belongs to those who prepare for it, and in the realm of AI, preparation begins with understanding. Embracing machine learning and deep learning is no longer optional; it's imperative for those wishing to thrive in a digital future where AI plays a central role.

Natural Language Processing Applications

As we dive into the rapidly advancing world of emerging AI technologies, natural language processing (NLP) stands as a beacon of transformation that reshapes the modern workplace. With the ability to understand, interpret, and generate human language, NLP applications offer a wide array of opportunities and solutions across various industries. At the heart of this endeavor lies the human aspiration to communicate seamlessly with machines, creating an ecosystem where technology understands and serves human needs with unprecedented precision.

Consider the customer service sector, where NLP tools have revolutionized how businesses engage with their clients. Chatbots powered by NLP can handle vast volumes of inquiries, providing timely and accurate responses, often without human intervention. This not only improves customer satisfaction but also frees up human resources for more complex tasks that require critical thinking and empathy. Moreover, language models can analyze customer feedback in multiple languages, providing companies with insightful data on customer needs and preferences.

In parallel, NLP is making inroads into healthcare. By enabling computers to comprehend and analyze clinical notes and patient records, health systems can extract valuable insights that inform patient care. For instance, predictive models can alert medical professionals to potential complications based on historical patient data. Additionally, NLP-driven virtual assistants can support medical staff by automating routine documentation and facilitating patient interactions, ultimately improving health outcomes.

In the realm of business operations, NLP applications are diverse and far-reaching. Intelligent document processing allows organizations to automate the extraction and categorization of data from unstructured documents. This capability streamlines workflows, enhances efficiency, and minimizes manual errors, thereby optimizing resource allocation. Managers and leaders can make informed decisions swiftly, backed by comprehensive data analysis facilitated by these advanced tools.

Marketing and sales teams also benefit tremendously from NLP technologies. Sentiment analysis, a subset of NLP, empowers companies to gauge public opinion on social media and other platforms, enhancing branding strategies. By understanding consumer sentiment in real-time, companies can pivot marketing campaigns and tailor messages to resonate more deeply with their target audiences, driving engagement and conversions.

In education, the potential of NLP is particularly inspiring. Language processing tools can assist educators in personalizing learning experiences, assessing student performance through essay analysis, and even providing support for language learners. By recognizing patterns in student submissions, NLP applications can offer customized feedback, enhancing the individual's learning journey and promoting better educational outcomes.

The financial sector, continuously on the leading edge of technological adoption, leverages NLP for everything from regulatory compliance to fraud detection. By sifting through complex legal documents and financial transactions, NLP models can flag potentially fraudulent activities and ensure adherence to regulatory standards. This proactive approach not only protects institutions but also fosters greater trust and transparency with clients.

The applications of natural language processing also extend into creative fields. Writers, designers, and content creators use NLP tools to assist with brainstorming, content generation, and editing. By analyzing linguistic styles and preferences, these tools can suggest improvements, generating innovative ideas that push creative boundaries. Thus, NLP acts as a collaborative partner, enhancing human creativity rather than overshadowing it.

One of the most exciting prospects of NLP is its role in bridging language barriers. Machine translation services are more accurate and contextually aware than ever, facilitating global communication across an array of languages. By enabling smooth interaction in multinational settings, these applications promote inclusivity and diversity, enriching workplace culture and business opportunities.

However, incorporating NLP into the workplace is not without challenges. Ethical considerations, such as data privacy and the mitigation of algorithmic bias, remain pivotal in ensuring the responsible development and deployment of these technologies. It is crucial for leaders and innovators to remain vigilant, actively addressing these concerns to foster an equitable digital landscape.

For business leaders and tech enthusiasts, the strategic integration of NLP can be a transformative move. It involves not only adopting the latest technologies but also reimagining organizational processes to harness these capabilities effectively. The journey towards an AI-driven workplace necessitates continuous learning, adaptability, and a forward-thinking mindset, cultivating an environment where human talent and artificial intelligence coexist harmoniously, driving innovation and growth.

As we look towards the future, the impact of natural language processing on the workplace is poised to grow exponentially. By aligning technological advancements with human values and aspirations, we can unlock unprecedented potential, creating a resilient and prosperous landscape that thrives on the synergy between human creativity and artificial intelligence.

This convergence of technology and humanity, facilitated by NLP, is not just a vision of tomorrow; it is an endeavor unfolding today. Embracing this evolution with curiosity and intent, individuals and organizations alike can navigate the complexities of the AI era, leading to enriched experiences, insights, and opportunities.

Chapter 4:
Redefining Human-Machine Collaboration

The intertwining of human ingenuity and artificial intelligence has ushered in a transformative era where collaboration transcends traditional boundaries. As we reevaluate the dynamics between humans and machines, a profound synergy emerges, characterized by a harmonious blend of analytical prowess and emotional intelligence. This juxtaposition allows machines to handle complex calculations and data processing while humans provide intuition, creativity, and ethical oversight. As businesses and industries adapt to this shift, the advantages of human-AI partnerships become increasingly apparent: enhanced productivity, innovative problem-solving, and the democratization of decision-making processes. Embracing this new paradigm not only augments capabilities but also propels organizations toward unprecedented growth and innovation. The challenge and opportunity lie in redefining roles and responsibilities, fostering an environment where the strengths of both humans and machines are leveraged fully, laying the foundation for a future where collaboration becomes the engine of progression. By prioritizing adaptability and continuous learning, professionals can harness the potential of AI, ensuring that this partnership remains a source of empowerment and advancement.

Synergy Between Humans and AI

In an age where technology evolves at an unprecedented rate, the concept of synergy between humans and AI isn't just a far-off possibility; it's a necessity that companies must embrace to thrive. It's about combining the analytical and swift calculating capabilities of AI with the nuanced understanding and emotional intelligence of humans. The convergence of these two forces can create a collaborative environment that not only improves efficiency but also opens avenues previously unexplored by either humans or machines working alone.

This synergy marks a transformative shift in the way we perceive roles within the workplace. Consider the dynamic between a jazz musician and their instrument. On its own, the saxophone is devoid of rhythm, a mere collection of metal pieces. But in the hands of a skilled musician, it tells stories, evokes emotions, and communicates complex ideas through harmonious notes. Similarly, AI can be the instrument that amplifies human creativity and decision-making processes, allowing us to push boundaries and explore new paths.

The potential of human-AI collaboration is vast, offering opportunities for personalization across various sectors. In healthcare, for instance, AI algorithms can analyze volumes of medical data at lightning speed, offering insights that would take a human far longer to process. When these insights are then interpreted through the empathetic lens of a healthcare professional, patient care becomes highly personalized, potentially leading to better outcomes.

In the business realm, AI can handle vast amounts of data, discern patterns, and even predict trends. But it's the human touch—understanding market nuances, cultural sensitivities, and the motivations driving customer behavior—that transforms these AI-driven insights into actionable strategies. With AI managing the heavy lifting of data analysis, humans are afforded more time to innovate and undertake strategic thinking, fostering an environment where creativity can flourish.

The educational sector can also benefit immensely from this synergy. AI systems are capable of tailoring educational content to match individual learning paces and styles, offering students a personalized learning experience. However, the need for educators remains crucial, as they provide context, inspiration, and motivation— a human touch that AI cannot replicate. By integrating AI into the classroom, educators can focus more on fostering critical thinking and less on administrative tasks.

Despite these advances, achieving true synergy between humans and AI isn't without its challenges. Trust remains a fundamental hurdle. Organizations and individuals must trust that AI systems are accurate, unbiased, and secure. Transparency in AI decision-making processes is essential to build this trust and encourage widespread adoption.

Another challenge lies in seamlessly blending AI systems into existing workflows. For synergy to be effective, humans and AI must operate within a framework that accentuates the strengths of both. This requires careful design and implementation of AI systems, along with ongoing training and adaptation. As technology evolves, so must our understanding and use of it.

The path to synergy involves continuous learning and adaptation. Organizations must cultivate a workforce that's ready and eager to embrace AI. This means investing in training programs that focus on both technical skills and new ways of thinking about problem-solving and innovation.

Moreover, from a managerial perspective, leaders must champion these changes while remaining open and communicative about the role and benefits of AI. This involves not just operational changes, but a cultural shift as well, reimagining roles and responsibilities to accommodate new paradigms in human-machine collaboration.

As AI becomes increasingly capable of deep learning and autonomous decision-making, the role of human oversight becomes vital. Ensuring ethical considerations and human values are embedded in AI's design and implementation is crucial. By guiding AI with a robust ethical framework, we can ensure that its development and use enhance rather than compromise our collective values.

Ultimately, the synergy between humans and AI holds the promise of transforming industries by implementing hybrid models of work that multiply productivity and creativity. The organizations that recognize and harness this potential will likely lead in innovation and efficiency, crafting workplaces that are as dynamic as the technologies that drive them.

This collaborative approach to work—this synergy—not only augments human capabilities but also challenges us to rethink the very fabric of the workplace. It asks us to envision a future where humans and machines don't just coexist but work together to unlock new dimensions of possibilities. It's a future built on mutual support, where each party's strengths are harnessed to overcome weaknesses, and where the pursuit of knowledge and improvement is endless. Such a future promises to redefine not only how we work but how we think about work itself.

The potential for the synergy between humans and AI extends beyond productivity gains. It invites us to redefine our understanding of intelligence, expanding it to include not only human intellect but also the unique cognitive processes that machines can contribute. Together, humans and AI can form a partnership that advances knowledge, fosters innovation, and ultimately creates a better world for all. This harmony will not occur naturally or automatically; it will require conscious effort and intention. But as we strive toward this future, the opportunity to reshape the world of work in unprecedented ways has never been more within our grasp.

Advantages of Human-AI Partnerships

The collaboration between humans and artificial intelligence has ushered in a new era of unprecedented opportunities and capabilities. In this landscape, the advantages of human-AI partnerships become strikingly evident as businesses aim to leverage both human creativity and machine efficiency. The modern workplace, with its rapidly evolving needs and challenges, seems tailor-made for such synergistic alliances.

First and foremost, AI complements human capabilities by taking over mundane, repetitive tasks, thereby freeing up human workers to focus on more complex, strategic problems. Consider, for instance, the analytics sectors where AI-driven models can process enormous data sets at incredible speeds. This ability not only enhances productivity but also allows human analysts to dedicate their time to interpreting and strategizing over the insights gleaned. The human touch—and its knack for intuition and strategic thinking—works hand in hand with AI's data-crunching proficiency, creating a partnership where each amplifies the other's strengths.

The partnership of humans and AI also paves the way for innovation, as it gives rise to creative solutions that might not have been achieved independently by either. AI can explore vast solution spaces quickly and hypothesize new combinations or alternatives, while humans bring in the contextual understanding and creativity necessary to adapt these hypotheses for real-world application. Take, for instance, the field of medicine, where AI can sift through countless research studies and genetic data, but it requires the expertise of medical professionals to decide the best course of action for a specific patient's needs. Through such collaboration, innovative treatments and methodologies can emerge that neither human ingenuity nor AI alone could predict.

Furthermore, AI's ability to learn from and adapt to its environment allows for a continuation of growth beyond initial deployment. Human counterparts play a crucial role in guiding this learning, ensuring that AI systems remain aligned with ethical standards and organizational goals. Such a partnership is indispensable in industries like finance, where real-time decision-making can have monumental impacts. Here, AI's speed is matched by human oversight, ensuring that decisions adhere to ethical considerations while optimizing for efficiency and profitability.

One significant advantage of these partnerships is the enhancement of decision-making processes. When humans and AI collaborate, the decision-making process becomes more reliable and swift, as machines provide data-driven insights that are backed by statistical evidence and historical trends. Conversely, human decision-makers can address aspects of judgment, ethical concerns, or side effects that AI might overlook. This creates a thorough and balanced approach to solving complex problems.

Moreover, human-AI partnerships pave the way for personalization at scale—an achievement that was previously inconceivable. In the realm of customer service, for example, AI algorithms analyze customer behavior patterns to generate personalized experiences that cater to individual preferences. While AI handles the data analysis, human workers can focus on developing empathetic and meaningful customer interactions that build trust and loyalty. This dual approach leads to higher customer satisfaction and retention rates.

Despite the transformative advantages of these partnerships, challenges remain. For such collaborations to reach their full potential, there must be a symbiotic relationship where humans and AI understand their roles and capabilities in depth. This necessitates a shift towards continuous learning and adaptation in workplaces, where humans must become proficient in working alongside AI, understanding its outputs, and interpreting its predictions with nuance and responsibility.

In organizations that champion a culture of innovation and openness, AI becomes a partner, not a competitor. The integration of AI has the potential to transform workplace culture by encouraging diversity of thought and inclusivity, as diverse teams bring varied perspectives on how to best utilize AI tools. Such a culture fosters environments where human creativity and machine capabilities coalesce, leading to groundbreaking discoveries and unparalleled efficiency.

A fundamental consideration in these partnerships is the democratization of AI technologies. By making AI tools accessible to non-technical workers, organizations can broaden the scope of innovation and empowerment. This democratization ensures that valuable insights are not locked away in specialized teams but are available throughout the organization, allowing broader participation and contribution to AI-driven projects. This approach not only helps integrate AI into various business functions but also encourages a more equitable distribution of opportunity and skills development within the workforce.

Across industries, the advantages we witness in human-AI partnerships confirm their pivotal role in shaping the future of work. From enabling precision in manufacturing to revolutionizing customer experiences with personalized touchpoints, the synergy between human intellect and machine learning continues to redefine what is possible. However, the most profound promise of human-AI partnerships may lie not just in solving current problems but in shaping a world where collectively, society benefits from the insights and innovations born from this unique collaboration.

Chapter 5:
The Future of Work

As we step into an era shaped by extraordinary technological advancements, the future of work promises to be defined by rapid adaptation and unprecedented possibilities. Through the lens of AI, this future is not merely about automating tasks but about redefining the fabric of how we work and thrive. While predictions point towards increased collaboration between humans and intelligent systems, the essence will be in how adaptable we are to these shifts. Jobs rooted in creativity, emotional intelligence, and advanced technical expertise are expected to flourish, lifting industries and economies. Meanwhile, organizations must anticipate these trends, ensuring they align their strategic visions with emerging realities. In doing so, they harness the full potential of AI, driving innovation and fostering a workforce equipped to leverage these tools. This chapter explores this transformative journey, casting light on how we can prepare for and embrace a work culture that values human ingenuity alongside machine intelligence.

Predictions and Trends in the AI Era

As we look into the horizon, artificial intelligence stands poised to reshape the landscape of work with a gravity unprecedented since the Industrial Revolution. This is not mere hyperbole. From machinery that transformed manual labor to the digital tools that redefined how we compute, AI is radically altering the contours of commerce, communication, and production. The future is calling, and it's one that's deeply intertwined with the philosophies of AI-driven efficiencies and innovations.

One primary trend is the shift from conventional job roles to new, AI-augmented professions. Already, we're seeing the emergence of hybrid job positions where human insights and machine precision coalesce. Roles such as AI trainers, who help refine machine algorithms, and data ethicists, who ensure AI aligns with societal values, are becoming more prevalent. These new professions not only harness human creativity but leverage AI efficiency, creating collaborative space where each complements the other.

Moreover, we anticipate an increased demand for soft skills. Critical thinking, innovation, and emotional intelligence are gaining prominence in a workforce increasingly populated by AI technologies. While machines excel at data crunching and pattern recognition, the nuances of human empathy and ethical decision-making remain uniquely ours. As AI handles routine tasks, humans are left with the space to focus on creative problem-solving and strategic planning—areas where our innate capabilities still outshine any algorithm.

This AI diffusion won't occur in a vacuum. Organizations are likely to undergo structural changes, with flatter hierarchies and more cross-functional teams. Decision-making processes, once reserved for top-down management, will become more data-driven and democratized through AI insights. Employees, armed with AI tools, will make informed decisions swiftly, aligning company strategies with real-time data analysis. This responsive, agile business environment fosters a culture of shared leadership and collaborative innovation.

In the AI era, personalization will become the norm rather than the exception. Consumers and employees alike will expect tailored experiences. AI algorithms will continue to refine their understanding of individual preferences and behaviors, customizing everything from consumer products to professional development tracks. This level of personalization will not only enhance customer satisfaction but will also redefine employee engagement, offering a more customized career experience that aligns with personal values and goals.

Yet, with these advancements comes the perennial question of ethics and privacy. As AI systems integrate more deeply into the workplace, safeguarding data integrity and addressing biases in machine learning algorithms will be paramount. Businesses will need to commit to transparent AI practices that build trust with their clients and workforce. Ethical frameworks will become indispensable, guiding AI development and implementation to ensure that innovation does not outpace societal norms and human rights.

Looking ahead, collaboration between AI and human creativity will spur unprecedented innovation across industries. Sectors such as healthcare, education, and finance stand to benefit enormously from AI-driven advancements. In medicine, for instance, AI can assist in diagnosing diseases and personalizing treatment plans. In education, adaptive learning technologies are already tailoring instruction to meet the individual needs of students, enhancing educational outcomes at scale. The financial industry is utilizing AI to predict market trends and manage risks more effectively.

AI's predictive capabilities are another game-changer. Businesses will not only react to market trends but anticipate them. Predictive analytics, fueled by AI, will allow firms to optimize operations, manage supply chains efficiently, and align resources strategically. This predictive prowess could lead to smarter supply chain management, reducing waste and optimizing resource allocation, thereby boosting sustainability efforts across various sectors.

Furthermore, AI is set to enhance remote work capabilities profoundly. With the rise of advanced collaboration tools, distributed teams can interact seamlessly in virtual environments that feel almost tangible. AI-driven language processing will break down language barriers, fostering more diverse and inclusive workplaces. This remote work revolution will offer not just flexibility but will redefine workplace culture and geography, making talent truly global and accessible.

We also gaze into a future where lifelong learning becomes second nature. The rapid progression of AI technologies necessitates constant upskilling and reskilling, and educational paradigms are adapting. Micro-learning modules, easily digestible and accessible online, will fit into the busy lives of professionals seeking to stay ahead. Adaptive AI systems can provide customized learning experiences, identifying gaps in knowledge and offering targeted content to bridge these gaps in real time.

As AI continues to permeate the workplace, the economic landscape itself will be reshaped. We predict a rebalancing of industries and economies, where nations heavily investing in AI technologies may gain an economic edge. Global collaboration on AI development is likely to rise, organizing multinational coalitions focusing on AI ethics, innovation, and regulatory frameworks. This interconnected approach will be crucial for harmonizing AI advancements with global values.

In summary, the AI era promises to bring about both challenges and opportunities that necessitate a proactive approach. Businesses and individuals alike must embrace adaptability, creativity, and ethics in their journey. By preparing for these trends today, we equip ourselves not merely to survive but to thrive in tomorrow's ever-evolving landscape. In this brave new world, embracing AI's potential while strengthening our human values ensures progress that is informed not just by technology, but by compassion and vision.

What Jobs Will Thrive

As we stand on the threshold of unprecedented technological change, many wonder which jobs will withstand the test of time in an AI-driven world. The good news is that while artificial intelligence reshapes industries, it also paves the way for new opportunities and revitalizes existing roles. Those who embrace adaptability, creativity, and emotional intelligence are well-equipped to thrive in this transformative era.

First and foremost, roles that emphasize uniquely human traits such as empathy, creativity, and critical thinking are less likely to be automated. This includes occupations in healthcare, where the delicate balance of human touch and advanced machinery is indispensable. Nurses, therapists, and social workers are prime examples of jobs where the ability to connect on a personal level remains pivotal.

Moreover, creative professions like writers, artists, and designers are set to flourish. AI can generate basic artistic concepts, but it lacks the nuanced perspective and cultural context that human creativity brings to life. As AI tools evolve, they will increasingly serve as collaborative partners, freeing humans from repetitive tasks and allowing them to focus on innovation and originality.

In the realm of technology, roles centered around AI management and oversight will gain prominence. Professionals who can bridge the gap between technical and non-technical teams and translate business requirements into AI solutions are in high demand. This includes AI ethicists, data analysts, and AI strategy consultants. Their expertise ensures that AI tools are deployed responsibly and align with corporate goals.

Teaching and educational roles are also expected to thrive. In a world where continuous learning is essential, educators who facilitate adaptive learning environments will see increased demand. These professionals will employ AI as a tool to tailor educational experiences, catering to diverse learning styles while maintaining the interpersonal interactions that foster genuine understanding and growth.

Additionally, sustainable careers in environmental science and renewable energy promise growth. As AI aids in modeling climate patterns and optimizing energy usage, professionals in these fields will harness technology to address pressing ecological challenges. This dynamic interplay between AI and sustainability is crucial for fostering a healthier planet.

Jobs in cybersecurity will become ever-more crucial, as AI introduces intricate systems that need safeguarding from cyber threats. Cybersecurity professionals will be at the forefront of protecting data privacy and security, requiring a combinational skill set of technological acumen and strategic foresight.

Customer experience roles are expected to expand too. Even though AI significantly enhances data collection and customer insights, individuals skilled at interpreting this data to forge authentic customer connections will be invaluable. Personalized service remains a differentiator in brand loyalty, and human-driven customer engagement is irreplaceable.

The agricultural sector is also poised for significant transformation. As AI enhances precision farming techniques, agronomists and specialists will leverage technology to improve crop yield and sustainability. This evolution will create hybrid roles where traditional expertise is complemented by technological proficiency.

In logistics, supply chain managers who integrate AI tools for optimized planning and operations will thrive. Efficient supply chains require not only automation but also human oversight to adapt to unforeseen disruptions. Professionals who excel in these areas enhance operational resilience and agility.

Lastly, freelance and gig economy roles are seeing a revival spurred by AI advancements in connectivity and productivity. As more professionals seek flexibility, AI tools provide the infrastructure to support diverse work arrangements, from digital marketing to virtual consulting. This shift allows individuals to carve niches in the expansive digital landscape.

Ultimately, the future of work is not about AI replacing human jobs but about collaboration. The potential for human creativity and AI-enabled efficiencies can lead to enriched roles and fulfillments. It's about understanding these shifts and preparing today for the possibilities of tomorrow.

Success in the AI era will depend on the ability to continuously learn, adapt, and leverage AI as an ally rather than a threat. By cultivating skills that emphasize our uniquely human capabilities, we'll ensure a harmonious coexistence between human labor and machine intelligence. As we navigate these changes, a proactive mindset will unlock opportunities that once seemed out of reach.

Chapter 6:
Reshaping Skillsets for an
AI-Driven World

The AI-driven landscape demands a shift in our professional skillsets, compelling us to harness a blend of technical acumen and uniquely human abilities. As automation transforms traditional roles, the value of creativity, emotional intelligence, and strategic thinking surges. Workers who adapt by acquiring digital fluency, data literacy, and collaborative skills will find themselves thriving amidst the change. Lifelong learning becomes not just an advantage but a necessity, as job frameworks continuously evolve. This continual cycle of learning and adaptation ensures that professionals remain relevant, enhancing their ability to leverage AI tools effectively. By fostering a skillset that embraces both complexity and adaptability, we don't just survive the AI revolution; we ride its wave toward new horizons of innovation and opportunity.

Skills in Demand in the AI Era

In the rapidly evolving landscape of an AI-driven world, it's clear that the skillsets required for success are undergoing significant transformation. The traditional competencies that once guaranteed employability are being augmented, and in some cases, replaced by new capabilities that align with the unique demands of today's technological advancements. As organizations integrate AI across operations, the ability to adapt, learn, and evolve becomes critical.

Workers and leaders alike must cultivate new skills to harness the full potential of AI technologies.

At the forefront of these changes is the burgeoning need for data literacy. In an era where data is regarded as the new oil, the ability to effectively gather, analyze, and interpret large datasets has become indispensable. Employees who can navigate data analytics not only help in making informed decisions but can strategically leverage insights to drive innovation and efficiency. As AI technologies like machine learning and big data analytics mature, proficiency in interpreting complex datasets transforms from a niche ability into a core skill.

The surge in AI applications has also amplified the importance of technical proficiency. This doesn't necessarily mean everyone must become a software engineer or data scientist, but a baseline understanding of how AI systems function, including their limitations and potential biases, is crucial. Professionals across sectors must familiarize themselves with fundamental AI concepts, enabling them to collaborate effectively with technology teams and make informed strategic decisions. Moreover, the demand for AI talent continues to increase, and skills in programming languages like Python, and expertise in AI frameworks, remain highly sought after.

Equally significant is the rise of skills in human-machine collaboration, an area many might overlook. As AI systems take on more sophisticated roles, understanding how to work alongside these technologies becomes a key competency. This involves not just technical acumen but the ability to intuitively interact and communicate with AI systems, ensuring that their integration is seamless and their output is maximized. An effective human-AI collaboration often means that human intuition complements machine precision, creating a powerful synergy that enhances output and decision-making.

Yet, beyond the technical, the AI era is surprisingly reinforcing the value of certain human-centric skills. Creativity, for instance, remains a distinctly human trait that is hard for machines to replicate. Importantly, creative problem-solving isn't just about artistic endeavors; it involves innovative thinking and the ability to approach problems from new angles—a skill that's increasingly valuable in developing AI solutions and addressing unforeseen challenges. Forward-thinking companies are investing in training that fosters innovation and lateral thinking, recognizing that creative minds often yield transformative breakthroughs.

Interpersonal skills are similarly gaining traction in this context. While machines are taking on more analytical and computational tasks, the ability to connect, communicate, and empathize with others is becoming even more critical. Whether it's managing an AI-driven project or working within a team that's utilizing AI tools, effective communication ensures that projects progress smoothly and that all stakeholders remain aligned. Emotional intelligence, therefore, is emerging as a crucial differentiator in leadership roles where guiding teams through digital transformation requires inspiration, motivation, and understanding.

Adaptability also stands out as an invaluable asset in an AI-infused work environment. With the continual evolution of technology, rigid adherence to traditional methods can quickly render organizations obsolete. Employees who remain flexible and open to change can help their companies navigate the complexities of AI advancement. Lifelong learning, closely linked to adaptability, is about cultivating a mindset that continuously seeks out new knowledge and opportunities for growth. This ability to embrace new information and remain curious allows professionals to stay ahead of the curve in their respective fields.

Another vital skill in the AI landscape is ethical reasoning. As AI systems grow more autonomous, ethical considerations surrounding their application become ever more pressing. Professionals equipped to foresee and dissect ethical dilemmas are paramount to ensuring that AI is implemented fairly, responsibly, and without bias. By fostering a culture of ethical awareness, organizations can preemptively address potential issues before they escalate, ensuring that innovation aligns with broader societal values.

Finally, in AI's ubiquitous adoption, strategic thinking emerges as a cornerstone of modern leadership. It involves anticipating AI's long-term impact on industry trends, aligning technological advancements with business goals, and making informed investments that drive sustainable growth. Leaders with strong strategic foresight can position their organizations to capitalize on AI opportunities while mitigating risks associated with rapid technological shifts.

The skills required for success in the AI era are as diverse as they are dynamic. From data literacy and technical proficiency to creativity and ethical reasoning, these competencies are reshaping the modern workforce. Professionals who strategically cultivate these skills position themselves at the forefront of innovation, ready to harness the transformative power of AI to drive their industries forward. As we continue to navigate this complex landscape, the ability to adapt, learn, and lead with empathy and insight remains our greatest asset.

Lifelong Learning and Adaptability

The rapid advancement of AI in today's world demands a rethinking of how we approach learning and skill development. We stand on the brink of an AI-driven future, one that isn't just transforming industries, but also reshaping our roles and opportunities. As professionals, business leaders, or tech enthusiasts, embracing a mindset of lifelong learning and adaptability is not just beneficial—it's essential. In a world where technology evolves at an unprecedented pace, the ability to learn continuously and adapt swiftly can be what sets us apart.

Adapting to an AI-driven landscape doesn't solely mean updating technical skills. It's about developing a holistic approach that combines technical knowledge with soft skills, critical thinking, and emotional intelligence. The nuances of working alongside AI systems highlight the need for skills such as creativity, problem-solving, and strategic vision, requiring human competencies that machines can't replicate. These skills enable us to interpret data insights and make decisions that balance logic with empathy. The integration of AI necessitates a workforce adept at leveraging human uniqueness and technological precision in tandem.

The concept of lifelong learning has been around for decades, but its significance has magnified in this AI renaissance. No longer confined to traditional academic settings, learning today is about curating personal and professional growth through diverse channels. From online courses to collaborative workshops, learning is pervasive, transcending the classroom. The rise of digital platforms offers unparalleled access to knowledge and skills, allowing individuals to tailor their learning paths to suit their needs and aspirations in real-time. The fluid nature of AI demands we perpetually evolve, with each update or breakthrough representing a learning opportunity. A formal education, while important, is only a starting point in this journey of continuous growth.

Adapting to the AI age requires a proactive stance on career development, demanding individuals constantly assess and redefine their career trajectories. In this dynamic environment, flexibility is key as the demand for certain skills can shift rapidly. Jobs of the past might evolve into roles we haven't even imagined yet. Being prepared to pivot, to change direction or focus swiftly in response to market needs, ensures not only survival in the workforce but the potential to thrive. Emphasizing adaptability, resilience, and agility allows professionals to navigate uncertainties with confidence.

The responsibility of fostering a culture of lifelong learning and adaptability extends beyond individuals. Organizations play a critical role in supporting their workforce through initiatives that promote continuous education and skill enhancement. Companies that encourage personal development demonstrate a commitment to their employees' growth. They understand that an adaptable workforce is better poised to leverage AI's transformative potential, driving innovation and performance. Providing resources such as training programs, mentorship, and learning incentives ensures teams are equipped to excel in AI-augmented roles.

Moreover, today's business leaders must lead by example, embodying a commitment to lifelong learning themselves. Demonstrating curiosity and a willingness to evolve can inspire their teams to do the same. Leaders who prioritize learning cultivate environments where employees feel valued and motivated to contribute more profoundly. This kind of leadership fosters an organizational culture that celebrates exploration and knowledge sharing, crucial elements in thriving amidst AI-driven changes. It establishes a foundation where continuous improvement is embedded into the company's ethos.

In parallel, governments and educational institutions bear the responsibility to recalibrate their approaches towards education and skill-building to align with the demands of an AI-centric world. Policy-makers must facilitate frameworks that emphasize agility in learning, ensuring curricula remain relevant and forward-thinking. Educational systems must nurture not just technical expertise but also interdisciplinary programs that bridge the gap between AI capabilities and human potential. There is an urgent need for collaborative efforts that include academia, industry, and policy-making bodies to prepare current and future generations to meet the challenges of an AI-driven future head-on.

Technology will continue to evolve, and so will the complexities of the workplace. Therefore, developing a habit of lifelong learning and adaptability is not merely a choice—it is an imperative. The journey involves recognizing the value of continuous development and being willing to embrace new learning paradigms. As we master the art of navigating perpetual change, we craft our roles in the AI-enhanced world. Embracing this mindset not only paves the way for personal success but also contributes to a more dynamic, innovative, and resilient global workforce.

Chapter 7:
Overcoming Challenges in AI Implementation

Tackling the hurdles of AI implementation requires a strategic blend of technical insight and human judgment, transforming challenges into opportunities for innovation. Navigating ethical concerns demands robust frameworks that prioritize fairness and transparency, ensuring systems respect privacy and rights. To curb bias in AI, organizations should invest in diverse datasets and inclusive design teams, constantly refining algorithms to mirror real-world complexities. The road isn't straightforward, and resistance arises from technological, cultural, and operational dimensions. Yet, by fostering an adaptive mindset and fostering cross-disciplinary collaboration, leaders can demystify AI, aligning it with organizational goals while building trust in technology's potential. Embracing these challenges not only propels businesses forward but also sets a precedent for responsible AI use, paving the way for sustainable growth and transformation in an AI-driven era.

Addressing Ethical Concerns

As artificial intelligence (AI) continues to weave itself into the fabric of our workplaces, the ethical concerns surrounding its implementation deserve a pivotal spotlight. AI offers promising solutions to many business challenges, yet it also ushers in complex, moral quandaries that cannot be ignored. Ethical considerations in AI aren't just academic musings; they're real-world issues with significant implications for businesses, society, and everyday life.

First and foremost, there's the concern of transparency. In a world increasingly guided by algorithms, understanding the "why" and "how" behind AI-driven decisions becomes crucial. When AI systems make decisions about hiring, lending, or medical treatments, the rationale behind these decisions must be clear. This necessity emerges not only for regulatory compliance but also to ensure trust. Without transparency, trust in AI systems can erode, leading stakeholders to question their fairness and accuracy.

Linked closely to transparency is the principle of accountability. As AI systems take on responsibilities traditionally held by humans, determining accountability becomes more challenging. If an AI system errs, who is responsible? The developer, the operator, or the AI itself? Acknowledging these questions, businesses must ensure that accountability structures are in place to handle AI-induced errors or failures effectively.

Confidentiality is another ethical frontier in AI. AI systems process massive amounts of data, often containing personal or sensitive information. Ensuring that this data is handled with the utmost respect for privacy is a moral obligation. This requires robust data governance frameworks to prevent unwanted exposure or misuse of personal data. The ethical handling of data offers a lifeline to data subjects, ensuring their rights and dignity are upheld.

Moreover, bias in AI cannot be overlooked. Without careful monitoring, AI systems can perpetuate and even exacerbate existing biases present in the data from which they learn. An overt display of this bias can result in discriminatory outcomes, affecting hiring practices, lending rates, and law enforcement, among others. Ensuring AI fairness requires a commitment across all development stages to frequently audit, test, and revise algorithms with diverse teams.

One might argue that as AI takes on more roles within organizations, the risk of dehumanization arises. Here, the challenge lies in ensuring that technology enhances rather than overshadows the human element. In customer service, for instance, while AI can streamline responses and provide valuable insights, it's essential that human empathy and interaction remain central where needed. Balancing AI's efficiency with the irreplaceable human touch becomes a testament to intentional ethical design.

Then there's the unavoidable issue of job displacement. As AI automates tasks and redefines workflows, it brings about concerns surrounding economic inequality and job security. The solution isn't avoiding AI, but rather equipping the workforce with the skills needed to thrive alongside it. Fostering continuous learning and adaptability within the workforce is not just ethically sound; it's a business imperative in an AI-driven world.

Ethical AI implementation also calls for inclusivity. A diverse AI development team can spot potential biases and ethical pitfalls that a homogenous group might overlook. This means that AI projects should prioritize diverse perspectives and experiences to ensure equitable outcomes across the board. Inclusivity becomes not only an ethical choice but a strategic advantage that leads to richer insights and more balanced systems.

Aligning AI systems with broader societal goals is non-negotiable. For instance, ensuring that AI systems contribute positively to environmental sustainability can be a significant ethical leverage point. By designing AI tools that promote resource efficiency and waste reduction, businesses don't just comply with regulations; they contribute to a sustainable future.

Finally, promoting transparency in communication around AI capabilities and limitations contributes to managing expectations realistically. Businesses must be forthright about what their AI systems can achieve and where they might fall short. Transparent communication fosters trust and aligns stakeholder expectations with actuality, paving the way for smoother AI integration.

Addressing ethical concerns in AI implementation is an ongoing journey. As technology evolves, so too do the challenges and opportunities it presents. By grounding AI strategies in strong ethical frameworks, businesses can navigate the complex landscape of AI implementation responsibly and sustainably, ensuring that this powerful tool serves humanity's interests at large.

Mitigating Bias in AI Systems

In the rapidly evolving landscape of artificial intelligence (AI), addressing bias within AI systems stands out as one of the most pressing challenges. As organizations increasingly rely on AI for decisions impacting hiring, lending, law enforcement, and healthcare, eliminating bias takes on a critical importance. Biases in AI systems can arise from multiple sources, including biased training data, flawed algorithms, or human oversight. Though the roots of this issue are complex, the implications are far-reaching, affecting the fairness, accuracy, and reliability of AI systems.

Understanding the mechanics of bias begins with acknowledging the data used in training AI. Often, these datasets reflect historical biases and societal prejudices, resulting in AI systems perpetuating or even exacerbating discrimination. A crucial first step in mitigating bias is curating datasets that are representative and diverse. Organizations must ensure their data collection processes include a wide array of demographic groups, perspectives, and contexts. This step helps in crafting a foundation where bias is minimized, allowing the AI to learn patterns that are fairer and more inclusive.

Aside from data, the algorithms themselves may introduce bias. Algorithms are not inherently intelligent; they follow the instructions they're given based on the data they process. To mitigate algorithmic bias, developers and engineers need to be vigilant in assessing how these algorithms function and adapt over time. Implementing fairness metrics during model development can help in regularly evaluating the impact of AI decisions on various demographic groups. These metrics encourage the design of systems that account for equity, ensuring that AI applications serve all users impartially.

Moreover, transparency in AI systems is vital for identifying and correcting biases. Stakeholders, including developers, users, and affected communities, need access to AI's decision-making processes to audit and challenge biased outcomes. Explainable AI, which emphasizes models that offer clear insights into their workings, plays a pivotal role here. By making AI's processes understandable, we create opportunities for stakeholders to identify where biases may sneak into analyses and decisions and take corrective actions before these biases cause harm.

Ensuring diverse teams are involved in AI development is another practical strategy. Human biases often seep into technology through developer blind spots. Thus, it's crucial that teams creating AI systems come from varied backgrounds and possess diverse experiences. This diversity can introduce multiple viewpoints, leading to more rounded AI solutions that consider a wide spectrum of potential biases and are more equipped to address them proactively than homogeneous teams.

Collaboration between technologists and social scientists is equally important. While developers understand the technicalities of AI, social scientists bring insights into human behavior, societal norms, and ethical considerations. Both perspectives are critical in creating AI systems that recognize and counteract bias. An interdisciplinary approach ensures AI not only performs tasks accurately but also aligns with ethical standards and promotes social fairness.

A paradigmatic shift towards continual learning and adaptation in AI systems can further aid bias mitigation. Traditional AI models often rely on static data, which leaves them susceptible to biases present at the time of data collection. By implementing continuous learning processes, these systems can adapt to new data forms, contexts, and understandings over time, providing a more resilient and fair model that can help counter biases arising from outdated information.

AI governance frameworks are becoming increasingly important as organizations strive to deploy these technologies ethically and responsibly. Establishing clear guidelines, policies, and standards for ethical AI use can provide a roadmap for mitigating bias. These frameworks should encompass data collection, processing methods, algorithm transparency, fair usage, and accountability measures. By adopting such frameworks, organizations send a strong message about their commitment to ethical AI practices, building trust with stakeholders and the broader public.

Investing in AI literacy is also a fundamental component of addressing bias. As AI technologies evolve, so must our understanding of their capabilities, limitations, and risks. Educating workforce and stakeholders about how AI works helps in identifying potential biases and understanding their impact. This education fosters a culture where questioning AI decisions is not only encouraged but expected, empowering employees to spot and rectify biased outcomes actively.

Regulatory compliance cannot be overlooked when tackling bias in AI systems. Laws and regulations around AI and data protection, such as the General Data Protection Regulation (GDPR) or proposed AI Act in various jurisdictions, push organizations to be more conscious of biases and privacy concerns. Adhering to these regulations not only reduces instances of bias but also ensures organizations remain on the right side of legal and ethical lines, thus maintaining their reputations.

Finally, it's essential to foster a sense of accountability among AI creators and users. When stakeholders understand the implications of AI bias and their roles in perpetuating or mitigating it, they become more conscientious about the systems they design and deploy. Accountability breeds responsibility, urging everyone involved to uphold fairness and equity at every stage of the AI lifecycle.

Ultimately, mitigating bias in AI systems transcends mere technical adjustments; it requires a cultural shift towards prioritizing fairness, transparency, and inclusivity in our digital tools. Organizations that champion these values and implement effective strategies to address bias are better positioned to build AI systems that enable a truly equitable future.

Chapter 8:
Strategies for Businesses in the AI Age

In a rapidly evolving AI landscape, businesses must adopt comprehensive strategies to thrive amidst technological disruption. By embracing digital transformation, companies can seamlessly integrate AI tools to streamline operations and enhance decision-making processes. This requires an agile mindset, where innovation is not just encouraged but embedded within the organizational culture. Businesses should consider recalibrating their models to leverage AI-driven insights, aligning them with core objectives to harness new opportunities. Crucially, fostering a collaborative environment where human intelligence complements AI capabilities will enable enterprises to maintain a competitive edge. Practically, this means investing in training programs that upskill the workforce, encouraging cross-disciplinary teams to drive creative solutions. As AI continues to reshape industries, organizations agile enough to pivot and align their goals with these technological advances will not only survive but set the standards in the AI age.

Embracing Digital Transformation

Digital transformation isn't just about technology adoption; it's a cultural shift that reimagines how a business operates and delivers value. In the AI age, embracing digital transformation means leveraging artificial intelligence to enhance processes, drive innovation, and derive actionable insights from data. Businesses that excel in this transformation position themselves to outperform competitors and meet rapidly evolving customer expectations. But how can a company begin this journey effectively?

One of the first steps in embarking on digital transformation is to cultivate a digital-first mindset across the organization. This involves breaking down silos and encouraging collaboration between IT and other departments. Integrating AI tools requires both technical understanding and alignment with business objectives. Establishing cross-functional teams can facilitate communication and ensure that AI initiatives address real business challenges rather than being a solution in search of a problem. Through interdisciplinary collaboration, businesses can foster innovation and adapt to changing market dynamics.

Building the necessary infrastructure is crucial for digital transformation in the AI age. Today, businesses have to invest in scalable and secure IT systems that can support advanced AI operations. This means not only upgrading systems but also ensuring data integrity and accessibility. Clean, well-organized data becomes the lifeblood of AI applications. Businesses need to focus on building data architectures that allow seamless data flow and real-time analytics, leading to informed decision-making processes.

Despite the appeal of AI-powered efficiencies, businesses must also address the human side of digital transformation. Skill development and change management play pivotal roles. The workforce needs adequate training and support to embrace AI. This involves upskilling employees to work alongside AI systems, focusing on skills that computers cannot easily replicate, like emotional intelligence, critical thinking, and complex problem-solving. Leadership should also play a part in reassuring employees, helping them understand that AI won't replace them but will augment their capabilities instead.

A strategic approach to digital transformation emphasizes creating value with AI beyond just operational efficiency. AI can help unlock new revenue streams, enable personalized customer experiences, and inspire new business models. For instance, predictive analytics can refine marketing strategies, identify growth opportunities, and enhance customer retention by offering tailored solutions. By leveraging AI in customer interactions, businesses can gather insights that inform product development, leading to more innovative and consumer-friendly offerings.

Businesses must also be prepared to navigate ethical considerations as they integrate AI into their operations. Transparency, fairness, and accountability should be at the forefront of AI-driven strategies. Organizations must develop a governance framework that ensures responsible AI usage. This framework should include guidelines and best practices for data privacy, bias mitigation, and ethical AI deployment. By adhering to ethical standards, businesses can build trust with stakeholders and set the stage for sustainable growth.

The journey toward digital transformation with AI isn't linear. Continuous evaluation and adaptation are essential as the AI landscape evolves. Businesses should implement feedback loops and performance metrics to assess the effectiveness of AI initiatives. This process involves gathering insights from AI performance to refine strategies and make necessary adjustments. Establishing a culture of learning and adaptability can help businesses stay agile in a rapidly changing environment.

Ultimately, embracing digital transformation is about driving forward-thinking change that aligns technological capabilities with organizational goals. Companies must envision a future where human ingenuity combined with AI enables breakthroughs and industry leadership. By fostering a culture that encourages experimentation and open-mindedness, businesses can harness AI's full potential, crafting a path that is not only innovative but sustainable and human-centric.

Innovating Business Models with AI

In the rapidly evolving landscape of the AI Age, businesses have no choice but to innovate their models if they want to thrive. AI is not just an optional add-on anymore; it's a transformative force that reshapes how businesses operate, create value, and interact with customers. Innovation, in this context, goes beyond mere adoption of AI technologies; it involves reimagining the very building blocks of business models to align with an AI-driven world.

Consider a traditional retail business. In the past, it might have focused on optimizing supply chains and enhancing customer experience through human interaction. With AI, however, the game changes. AI-powered tools can predict consumer behavior with remarkable accuracy by analyzing vast datasets, helping businesses to tailor their offerings in unprecedented ways. Personalized recommendations, dynamic pricing, and AI-driven inventory management are more than just buzzwords—they are fundamental shifts in how retail businesses can operate effectively and profitably in today's market.

Financial services also illustrate the potential for AI to innovate business models. Traditionally, these institutions relied on manual processes and human judgment to assess risk, approve loans, or detect fraud. But now, AI enables real-time analysis of financial data at scales impossible for humans alone. Risk assessments, for instance, become ultra-efficient, leveraging machine learning algorithms that continuously learn and adapt to new data. Moreover, AI-driven platforms can provide consumers with customized financial advice, reshaping the customer relationship from a transactional one to a more advisory role. This shift not only enhances customer satisfaction but also opens up new revenue streams.

Yet, innovation doesn't stop with customer interactions or internal processes. It's also about the emergence of entirely new business models that capitalize on AI's capabilities. Subscription and as-a-service models are becoming prevalent due to AI's predictive and adaptive nature. Take, for example, the concept of AI-as-a-Service (AIaaS), enabling businesses of various sizes to access sophisticated AI tools without hefty upfront investments. Companies can now innovate without developing proprietary technology in-house, significantly lowering the barrier to entry. This democratizes AI and fosters a more competitive and vibrant market landscape.

But the real triumph of AI in business model innovation lies in its ability to forge new value propositions. For example, AI empowers companies to shift from selling products to selling solutions. Consider a manufacturing company that transitions to offering predictive maintenance services through AI analytics, sparing customers costly downtime and enhancing machine longevity. This paradigm shift redefines the customer-company relationship and aligns business success with customer outcomes.

While the benefits are undeniable, integrating AI into business models is not without its challenges. Organizations often face cultural and structural barriers that impede innovation. Developing an agile mindset, where continuous experimentation and iteration are valued, becomes critical. This shift requires leadership that is ready to embrace the uncertainties of AI integration and an environment that encourages risk-taking and failure as part of the innovation process.

The ethical implications of AI-driven models cannot be overstated. Responsible use of AI involves maintaining transparency with stakeholders and ensuring the ethical treatment of data. Companies that innovate ethically set themselves apart by building trust with customers, creating long-term loyalty and brand resilience. A failure in this regard could not only impact customer trust but also invite regulatory scrutiny that can hinder innovation.

The transformative power of AI also invites new entrants into markets long dominated by established players. Startups leveraging AI technologies can compete effectively with traditional businesses, often overtaking them by offering superior, AI-based solutions and experiences. This disruption compels established companies to engage in a perpetual cycle of re-evaluation and adaptation of their business models.

Collaboration is another dimension of innovation with AI. By forming alliances with tech companies and AI specialists, traditional businesses can integrate cutting-edge AI solutions more swiftly. Such partnerships facilitate knowledge exchange and drive hybrid business models, where technology and industry expertise come together to deliver innovative solutions.

Lastly, the path to innovating business models with AI is highly iterative and requires a commitment to lifelong learning. As AI technologies evolve, so too must business models. This necessitates a learning culture where employees at all levels are continually upskilled and exposed to new AI-driven possibilities. Companies that prioritize learning and adaptability will undoubtedly be the ones that not only manage to survive in the AI Age but thrive.

In essence, AI is not merely a tool to improve existing business functions—it's a catalyst for creating new paradigms of value creation and capture. By integrating AI into the core of their business models, companies position themselves to unlock unprecedented growth opportunities and define the competitive landscape of the future.

Chapter 9:
AI in Decision-Making

As businesses strive for agility and precision in today's fast-paced environment, AI has emerged as a vital tool in the decision-making process. It's not just about automating tasks; AI provides an analytical backbone that enhances business strategies by utilizing massive volumes of data with unprecedented speed and accuracy. Companies can now harness AI to predict trends, optimize operations, and make informed strategic choices that were previously unimaginable. This transformation is reshaping the landscape, where data-driven decisions outpace instinctual choices, providing a competitive edge in complex markets. However, the successful integration of AI in decision-making demands a keen understanding of its capabilities and limitations. It requires leaders to cultivate a robust data culture, where insights are valued and acted upon, effectively bridging the gap between raw data and strategic action. Embracing AI doesn't mean relinquishing human intuition and creativity; rather, it complements these attributes, making decision-making processes more robust and future-ready. As organizations delve deeper into AI's potential, they stand at the forefront of an era where decisions increasingly rely on a harmonious blend of machine intelligence and human acumen, paving the way for a new age of innovation and efficiency.

Enhancing Business Strategies

In the ever-evolving landscape of modern business, leveraging AI in decision-making isn't just advantageous—it's essential. Companies no longer question if they should embrace AI; the focus has shifted to how they can best harness these technologies to fuel strategic growth and adaptability. Every business leader understands that strategic planning isn't a static endeavor. It requires a dynamic process where timely, data-driven decisions can make the difference between thriving and merely surviving.

AI offers unprecedented opportunities to enhance business strategies by providing insights that were previously unreachable. Through sophisticated data analytics, AI can identify patterns and trends that may not be apparent through traditional methods. This capability enables businesses to make proactive decisions that anticipate market shifts, customer behavior changes, and potential operational bottlenecks.

Consider an industry like retail. AI can analyze purchasing patterns with remarkable precision, predicting future trends and consumer preferences. This foresight allows retailers to adjust inventory before demand spikes or declines, optimizing the supply chain and reducing waste. Successful strategies can develop through real-time data integration into decision-making processes, ensuring competitive advantage.

Yet, leveraging AI to enhance business strategies requires more than just the deployment of technology. It demands a shift in organizational mindset. The most effective companies are those that foster a culture of innovation and encourage the adoption of AI tools across all levels of the organization. This cultural adaptation often begins with leadership who champion AI initiatives, understanding their potential to transform vision into reality.

Moreover, AI can streamline the process of evaluating strategic options. Decision-makers often face the challenge of choosing the best path amidst numerous possibilities. AI-driven simulations can model different scenarios, projecting the possible outcomes of each strategic choice. With these insights, leaders can weigh the potential risks and rewards of various strategies with unprecedented clarity, crafting plans that align with company goals and market conditions.

However, the implementation of AI in strategy needs careful consideration of ethical implications. Responsible AI use ensures decisions are made transparently and equitably, promoting trust among stakeholders. Companies must prioritize data privacy and fairness, setting the foundation for sustainable AI applications that align with ethical standards.

One of AI's most compelling contributions is its ability to personalize strategic approaches. Tailored strategies aren't limited to customer interactions but extend to internal business processes. AI can identify employee performance trends, suggesting personalized training and development programs. By aligning individual growth with business goals, companies can foster a workforce that is both skilled and motivated.

Furthermore, while AI offers vast potential in strategy enhancement, human intuition and expertise remain irreplaceable. The synergy between AI and human insight leads to superior strategic outcomes. This combination leverages AI's analytical prowess while considering human creativity and empathy, fostering strategies that resonate on both rational and emotional levels.

An essential aspect of enhancing business strategies with AI is iterating and refining those strategies based on continuous feedback. In the fast-paced AI era, static strategies quickly become obsolete. Companies must adopt a mindset of agility, where learning from each AI-driven insight becomes part of the strategic cycle. This iterative process ensures that the business remains adaptable and resilient in the face of ever-changing external environments.

The future of strategic planning lies in AI's integrative capabilities. AI systems that connect disparate data sources provide a comprehensive view of business operations, market conditions, and competitor activities. This holistic perspective is crucial for devising strategies that are not only innovative but also coherent and executable.

As businesses continue to integrate AI into their strategic frameworks, partnerships and collaborations are increasingly vital. Engaging with AI experts and technology partners can expedite the learning curve and deployment speed, allowing businesses to capitalize on AI's benefits more swiftly. Collaborative efforts foster innovation, pooling knowledge and resources to create more robust and impactful strategies.

In summary, AI is reshaping how businesses formulate and execute their strategies, embedding intelligence into every aspect of business planning. By harnessing AI, companies are equipped to anticipate and react to changes with agility and precision, ensuring long-term success. The road to enhancing business strategies with AI is one marked by opportunity, insight, and a shared vision of a future where human ingenuity and machine intelligence go hand in hand.

Data-Driven Decision Processes

In today's fast-paced business environment, data-driven decision processes are the backbone of successful strategic planning. Gone are the days when executives relied solely on intuition or historical precedent. Now, data and its efficient analysis enable businesses to make informed decisions that drive growth. Artificial Intelligence (AI) enhances this decision-making process by offering tools that can process vast amounts of data with remarkable precision and speed, transforming raw information into actionable insights.

AI's ability to process complex datasets has fundamentally changed how organizations approach decision-making. Consider a retail company navigating market fluctuations and customer preferences. In the past, understanding demand required extensive market research, which was often time-consuming and outdated by the time it was analyzed. With AI, decision-makers can access real-time data and trends to pivot strategies with agility and accuracy. This shift not only optimizes product offerings but also aligns marketing efforts directly with consumer behavior.

Machine learning, a subset of AI, plays a pivotal role in data-driven decision processes. It uses algorithms to identify patterns and predict future outcomes based on historical data. Companies that leverage machine learning can anticipate market shifts, customer needs, and internal process improvements. For example, in the financial sector, algorithms identify fraudulent transactions beyond the capabilities of human analysts, simultaneously protecting assets and assuring compliance.

Artificial Intelligence acts as a catalyst in transforming data into operational expertise. Businesses benefit from AI-driven analyses that uncover insights buried within the mountains of data they collect daily. These insights enable a level of precision previously unimaginable in forecasting and strategic planning. Autonomous driving systems are a practical application where real-time data analysis must inform split-second decisions, ensuring safety and efficiency on the road.

Among the tremendous advantages of AI in data-driven decision-making is predictive analytics. This tool comprises statistical techniques that analyze current and historical facts to forecast future events. Retailers use predictive analytics to determine inventory needs, optimizing supply chains for efficiency, and reducing costs. Meanwhile, healthcare providers predict patient admissions, allowing staff to allocate resources more effectively and improve patient outcomes.

Yet, as the potential of AI in decision processes grows, so does the complexity. Organizations must evolve to manage this intricate landscape effectively. This means investing in technology infrastructure and nurturing a workforce adept in data analytics and AI tools. Skilled data scientists and AI specialists are crucial, as their expertise transforms raw data into intuitive, easily digestible insights for stakeholders.

The essence of data-driven decision-making also lies in its adaptability. Unlike traditional systems, AI-enhanced systems can adjust to new information dynamically. This adaptability is essential in environments subject to frequent changes, such as financial markets or technology sectors. Real-time feedback loops provided by AI systems allow businesses to rapidly respond to external changes, fostering resilience and competitive advantage.

Furthering data-driven decisions, AI systems integrate seamlessly with existing databases, enabling organizations to leverage past data coupled with real-time inputs. Through this synergy, AI uncovers value at a granular level, facilitating decisions that optimize asset use, improve customer satisfaction, and drive bottom-line performance. For tech enthusiasts and business leaders, understanding these capabilities will be essential to harness AI's full potential.

Challenges persist, of course. One critical consideration is data quality. Without high-quality data, AI systems produce unreliable outcomes, potentially steering strategic decisions off course. Organizations must ensure robust data governance frameworks to maintain the integrity of information feeding AI systems. Implementing strong data validation processes and ensuring transparency are also essential elements of an effective data-driven strategy.

In summary, data-driven decision processes powered by AI represent a monumental shift in the strategic landscape. By enhancing an organization's ability to analyze data and predict outcomes, AI not only elevates decision-making effectiveness but also spurs innovation and improves operational efficiencies. As companies continue to embrace AI, the leaders of tomorrow will be those who adeptly leverage data-driven insights to anticipate change and capitalize on new opportunities.

Chapter 10:
The Impact of AI on
Organizational Culture

As artificial intelligence reshapes business landscapes, its influence on organizational culture is both profound and multifaceted. AI is not merely a tool; it's becoming woven into the fabric of workplace ethos, driving companies to rethink their values, norms, and practices. Organizations embracing AI-driven transformation often witness a shift towards a culture of innovation, where collaborative problem-solving and continuous learning become central tenets. The infusion of AI technologies encourages openness and adaptability, as teams are energized to experiment and iterate, learning from both successes and failures. This cultural evolution requires leaders to cultivate an environment that balances technological leverage with human-centric values, fostering trust and resilience amidst change. Essentially, AI is not only altering how businesses operate but also redefining what they stand for, steering them toward a future rich with potential and exploration.

Building an AI-Friendly Workplace Environment

The integration of artificial intelligence into the workplace signifies more than just a technological change; it marks a transformative shift in the organizational culture. Simply put, to build an AI-friendly workplace environment, businesses must foster a culture that's not only adaptive to these technological advances but also inclusive and human-centric. This transformation necessitates a thoughtful approach that balances innovation with the human touch.

Embedding AI into everyday operations requires a company-wide embrace of change. Management should lead by example, displaying openness to learning and experimenting with AI technologies. This sets the tone for a culture that values continuous improvement and innovation. Encouraging employees to participate in AI-related initiatives can demystify these technologies and integrate them seamlessly into their workflows.

Communication is a foundational pillar in establishing an AI-friendly environment. Transparent discussions about AI's role, its capabilities, and potential limitations are crucial. Employees need reassurance that AI aims to augment rather than replace human intelligence. Fostering open dialogues helps reduce resistance and builds trust, paving the way for smoother transitions.

Training and development programs are essential components of creating an AI-friendly workplace. These programs should be tailored to meet the diverse needs of employees, offering resources that range from basic AI literacy to advanced technical skills. While some team members may require only a fundamental understanding of AI, others—particularly those directly interacting with AI systems—will need more specialized training.

An inclusive culture is vital for leveraging AI's full potential. Diversity in teams brings varied perspectives that can lead to more innovative AI solutions. It's important to ensure that AI systems serve all users equitably, which requires diverse inputs during the development and refinement of these technologies.

Moreover, creating an adaptive workspace involves integrating AI tools that promote collaboration. AI can streamline communication, manage project workflows, and even suggest strategic directions based on data analysis. Tools that facilitate interaction and teamwork can help to break down silos, promoting a more interconnected and dynamic organizational structure.

Recognizing the human value within AI processes leads to more fulfilling work environments. By allowing AI to handle routine tasks, employees are freed to focus on more creative and strategic activities. This shift can enhance job satisfaction and lead to fresh opportunities for professional growth.

However, the ethical deployment of AI must remain a priority. Companies should establish clear policies governing AI use, addressing issues such as data privacy, job impacts, and decision transparency. By holding regular ethics reviews and engaging employees in these discussions, businesses can build a culture that respects human values while embracing AI benefits.

Feedback loops should be another cornerstone of an AI-friendly workplace. Regular assessments of AI implementation, soliciting feedback from users, and making iterative improvements create an environment of continuous advancement. Employees should feel empowered to voice concerns and contribute ideas to refine AI systems.

The journey toward a fully integrated AI environment is an ongoing process. It's vital to remain adaptable and responsive to emerging AI trends and technologies. By staying proactive, organizations can not only mitigate disruptions but also capitalize on the opportunities AI presents.

In conclusion, building an AI-friendly workplace is a multifaceted endeavor that necessitates a harmonious blend of technology and human-centered practices. It involves cultivating an environment where AI is viewed as a partner that enhances capabilities, fosters innovation, and respects the human element. Through this integration, organizations can not only thrive in the AI era but also emerge as frontrunners in their industries, equipped to face the future with confidence and agility.

Fostering a Culture of Innovation

The infusion of artificial intelligence (AI) into organizational culture is not just an upgrade—it's a transformation. As AI reshapes the workplace, fostering a culture of innovation becomes not merely a strategic advantage but a necessity. Organizations that effectively harness the potential of AI do so by cultivating an environment where creativity meets technology, ensuring that innovation thrives organically.

At the heart of fostering an innovative culture is the mindset shift AI necessitates; it's about moving from a process-centric approach to one that is more curiosity-driven and adaptable. This transformation often begins with leadership, who must champion the change by modeling a mindset open to continuous learning and experimentation. Leaders should encourage employees to explore AI tools not as a replacement for human ingenuity but as catalysts for new ideas and pathways.

To support this cultural shift, companies may benefit from creating cross-functional teams that include both tech-savvy individuals and those from diverse business backgrounds. The diversity in thought and experience can lead to novel interpretations and uses of AI, fueling a dynamic environment where innovation can flourish. Such teams are adept at seeing AI not just as a tool for efficiency but as a partner in creativity, capable of trialing radical new ideas without the limiting constraints of routine processes.

The implementation of AI provides a unique opportunity for businesses to break down silos and promote a collaborative spirit. When diverse teams work together on AI projects, they can cross-pollinate ideas, leading to innovative solutions that wouldn't emerge in isolation. For instance, when marketing collaborates with data science, customer insights can be transformed into highly personalized user experiences, thus fostering innovation at the intersection of disciplines.

Moreover, there's an intrinsic motivation for companies to mold their structures around a flexible, agile framework that accommodates rapid technological changes. One such approach is adopting agile methodologies alongside AI, enabling teams to iterate quickly on projects, learn from data-driven insights, and pivot strategies swiftly in response to findings. This culture of agility and responsiveness can drive continuous improvement and innovation.

While AI can automate mundane tasks, it simultaneously frees up human potential for more creative endeavors. An innovation-centric culture encourages employees to channel this available energy into generating ideas, exploring what-if scenarios, and pursuing ambitious projects that might have previously been sidelined. In such an environment, failure is not just tolerated but seen as a valuable learning step and an integral component of the innovation process.

Creating an ecosystem that supports innovation also involves recognizing and rewarding creativity. Forward-thinking organizations devise systems for acknowledging and celebrating innovative efforts, whether successful or not, reinforcing the notion that taking risks and pushing boundaries are integral to progress. This recognition can be fostered through incentives, but equally through a shared language and narrative that highlights stories of innovation within the organization.

A vital aspect of fostering such a culture is the continuous investment in learning and development. Curated training programs that focus both on technical skills and on nurturative soft skills, such as creativity and critical thinking, can empower employees to leverage AI tools effectively and innovatively. Learning platforms need to be accessible and engaging, encouraging self-directed learning as a norm rather than an exception.

Technology, including AI, evolves rapidly, and organizations must nurture a culture where staying informed and adapting is part of their DNA. Platforms that promote knowledge sharing across the organization can be instrumental, providing collaborative spaces—virtual or physical—where employees discuss trends, share insights, and even prototype new AI-driven ideas collectively.

All these efforts to create a culture of innovation should align with the organization's mission and values, ensuring that the pursuit of novelty does not overshadow the company's foundational goals or ethical principles. As AI continues to embed itself deeply into the fabric of the workplace, it offers both opportunities and challenges in equal measure, making it imperative to innovate responsibly.

In conclusion, building a culture of innovation in the AI era is not about implanting radical new ideas overnight. It requires a nuanced approach that blends leadership, diverse teams, agile methodologies, and continuous learning into a cohesive strategy that positions the organization to thrive in an AI-driven world. By fostering an environment where AI enables creativity and ideation, organizations ensure not only their survival but their leadership in the future's uncharted territories.

Chapter 11:
Leadership in the AI Era

As the AI era unfolds, the essence of leadership is being redefined with both urgency and opportunity at the forefront. Leaders now find themselves at the intersection of technology and humanity, tasked with guiding their organizations through unprecedented change and uncertainty. It's not just about understanding AI; it's about harnessing its potential while nurturing a culture that embraces innovation and resilience. AI-ready leaders must cultivate an agile mindset, able to pivot strategies and inspire teams amid the rapid transformations that AI heralds. Transparency, empathy, and ethical foresight remain pivotal as leaders aim to balance technological advancements with human-centered values. Developing leaders equipped for this landscape involves bridging technical acuity with emotional intelligence, making informed decisions that integrate AI capabilities seamlessly into business vision. The true test of leadership in this AI-driven world lies in the ability to navigate complex dynamics, fostering an environment where technology empowers human capabilities rather than diminishing them.

Developing AI-Ready Leaders

As the AI era transforms every facet of business operations, leadership must evolve alongside it. Today's leaders aren't just managing teams—they're navigating a landscape where artificial intelligence enhances capabilities, challenges traditional thinking, and reshapes decision-making processes. The art of leading now requires a robust understanding of technology, an authentic commitment to adaptability, and an unshakeable dedication to ethical considerations. Leaders who thrive in this era are those who can blend these elements into a coherent vision, steering their organizations with foresight and empathy.

At the core of developing AI-ready leaders is the ability to embrace change. Change is no longer episodic; it's continuous. As AI technologies advance and disrupt established protocols, leaders must be vigilant learners. The most successful leaders are those who prioritize knowledge acquisition—not just for themselves but for their teams. They create environments where learning is part of the organization's DNA, encouraging an ethos of perpetual skill enhancement. This means investing in training programs focused on AI literacy, hosting workshops that delve into emerging technologies, and fostering a culture where questioning the status quo is not just accepted but celebrated.

Moreover, being an AI-ready leader means understanding the intricate balance between human intuition and machine intelligence. While AI can sift through vast datasets, identifying patterns with speed and accuracy, it lacks the nuanced understanding of context and human emotion. Leaders need to cultivate this balance by reinforcing the importance of human judgment in AI-powered decision-making processes. They must guide teams in interpreting AI outputs, ensuring that the technological insights are grounded within human values and organizational objectives.

Equally, the ethical dimensions of AI use cannot be understated. The deployment of AI solutions comes with a slate of ethical questions concerning data privacy, algorithmic bias, and the societal impact of automation. Leaders prepared for the AI era must engage deeply with these issues, championing transparency and responsibility. They strive to establish frameworks that safeguard against ethical pitfalls, promoting practices that elevate AI's role as a tool for societal betterment rather than a mechanism for disparity.

Developing AI-ready leaders also requires honing distinct leadership skills—agility, resilience, and vision. Agility allows leaders to quickly pivot strategies in response to new AI developments. They must remain nimble, adjusting plans dynamically as technology evolves. Resilience defines a leader's capacity to endure setbacks that accompany innovation, fostering a mindset where failures are viewed as opportunities for growth and learning. Vision is crucial; leaders must articulate a clear roadmap where AI is not an add-on but is integrated into the organization's core strategies.

Leadership in the AI era extends beyond the walls of any organization. It encompasses building networks of collaboration across industries, joining forces to tackle the shared challenges and opportunities AI presents. Leaders must advocate for and participate in cross-sector dialogues, seeking alliances that enhance collective understanding and application of AI technologies. By fostering cooperation, they contribute to a global framework poised to harness AI for shared prosperity.

Furthermore, the emotional intelligence of leaders becomes increasingly pivotal. As AI handles more routine tasks, the human component becomes the differentiator in creating cohesive, motivated teams. Leaders need to excel in areas that AI can't replicate: empathy, inspiration, and the nurturing of workplace relationships. They should aim to be connectors—bridging the gap between digital capabilities and the human experience, ensuring that their teams feel valued and are driven by a sense of purpose.

A critical component of readiness is preparing for the unknown future. AI will undoubtedly bring unforeseen challenges, and leaders must cultivate a mindset that embraces uncertainty as an intrinsic part of progress. This means being proactive in scenario planning and engaging in strategic foresight initiatives, considering not just immediate technological impacts but also potential long-term societal changes. It's about building organizational resilience—developing structures and cultures that can withstand and adapt to unexpected shifts.

The journey to becoming an AI-ready leader is not a solitary endeavor. Mentorship and peer learning are invaluable. Leaders benefit from dialogues with experts from various fields, gaining insights that enrich their approaches to integrating AI. Facilitating peer learning networks within their organizations further strengthens leaders' capabilities and ensures that knowledge sharing becomes a part of the organization's fabric.

In conclusion, developing AI-ready leaders is an imperative that transcends mere technological expertise. It demands a holistic reimagining of leadership qualities to include a keen insight into technological advances, the courage to navigate ethical minefields, and a deep-seated belief in lifelong learning and human values. Leaders who can successfully guide their organizations through the AI era stand to unlock unprecedented levels of success and innovation, leaving a legacy that blends technological prowess with human integrity.

Navigating Change and Uncertainty

In the AI era, leaders confront an ever-evolving landscape, one that is often marked by unpredictability and constant change. For many, this represents a formidable challenge, yet it also offers a unique opportunity for growth and innovation. As AI technologies rapidly progress, so too must the leaders who guide organizations through this turbulent terrain. Navigating change and uncertainty demands a blend of vision, adaptability, and resilience—a dance that is as strategic as it is intuitive.

Change management is at the heart of effective leadership in today's AI-driven world. It's not merely about reacting to change but proactively shaping it. Leaders must foster a culture that embraces transformation rather than resists it. This involves cultivating an environment where experimentation is encouraged, and failure is considered a stepping stone to innovation. Such a mindset doesn't just facilitate smoother transitions; it also empowers teams to harness the full potential of AI.

The speed at which AI evolves can naturally incite trepidation among team members. Fear of obsolescence, anxiety over job security, and concerns about ethical implications are common sentiments. A leader's role in this context is twofold: to alleviate fears and to articulate a clear, forward-looking narrative that inspires confidence and commitment. Open communication channels are essential, enabling leaders to address concerns transparently and engage teams in the vision for the future.

Agility is a critical component in navigating the unpredictable currents of AI advancements. Leaders need to be nimble, ready to pivot strategies as new technologies emerge and business landscapes shift. An agile approach doesn't just prepare an organization for change; it embeds adaptability into its very fabric. This requires leaders to be continually learning, staying abreast of the latest AI developments, and understanding how these can be leveraged strategically.

It's undeniable that the intersection of AI and business strategy demands a rethinking of traditional leadership models. There's a necessity to move away from hierarchical structures towards more decentralized decision-making processes which can adapt swiftly to change. Empowering teams to make decisions can foster innovation and speed in response to AI-driven transformations. Leaders must trust their teams with responsibility and authority, acknowledging that collective intelligence often outpaces individual insight.

Moreover, the uncertainty that accompanies rapid technological evolution calls for a resilience-centric leadership style. Resilience isn't just about bouncing back from setbacks; it's about building defenses against potential disruptions before they occur. Leaders with a strong sense of resilience create organizations that remain robust amidst chaos and continued uncertainty. This capacity is nurtured through strategic foresight and scenario planning, enabling leaders to anticipate and prepare for a variety of future scenarios.

Strategic foresight involves envisioning multiple futures and crafting resilient strategies that can thrive under diverse conditions. It requires a mindset that's as comfortable in ambiguity as it is in certainty. By adopting such an approach, leaders can transform potential challenges into opportunities. They don't just react to change, they anticipate it, nudging their organizations to be first movers and innovators in the marketplace.

In the whirlwind of change that AI brings, emotional intelligence becomes an invaluable asset for leaders. Understanding and managing one's own emotions, as well as empathizing with others, helps in creating a supportive culture during transitions. Leaders who exhibit high emotional intelligence foster loyalty and retention, which are crucial in times of change. They understand that change isn't only a technical or strategic shift but a human one, involving real emotions and responses.

Being an AI-era leader means committing to lifelong learning—not only in the technical sense but in understanding the cultural and humanistic aspects of AI integration. By investing in their own development and that of their teams, leaders pave the way for a robust organizational learning culture. Learning isn't just about acquiring new knowledge; it's about learning how to learn, how to unlearn outdated methods, and how to foster a curiosity-driven mindset throughout the organization.

At the same time, navigating change and uncertainty requires a profound commitment to ethical stewardship. As AI systems become more prevalent, leaders must grapple with ethical dilemmas and work to establish guidelines that ensure the responsible use of technology. This includes addressing biases in AI algorithms and safeguarding data privacy, underscoring the need for a principled approach to AI governance.

In conclusion, leading in the AI era is as much about embracing the unknown as it is about leveraging the known. It is about balancing technological possibilities with human values, fostering a culture that celebrates adaptability and resilience. By doing so, leaders can not only navigate the inherent uncertainties of AI but also transform these challenges into groundbreaking opportunities. It's a journey of continuous transformation, where the leader's vision, courage, and commitment shape the future of their organization and the broader landscape in which it operates.

Chapter 12:
AI and the Global Economy

As AI continues to infiltrate the global economy, it acts as a catalyst for unprecedented transformation, reshaping industries and redefining economic paradigms. From automating routine tasks to bolstering decision-making processes, AI's economic implications are profound and multi-dimensional. Economies worldwide are witnessing shifts in competitive advantages as nations race to develop and harness AI technologies, leading to new forms of international collaboration and geopolitical dynamics. This technological surge influences not only economic output but also labor markets, sparking debates on employment, income distribution, and skill development. In this interconnected era, businesses and governments must collaborate, fostering innovation while addressing ethical and societal impacts. The challenge lies in ensuring these advancements promote equitable growth, empowering economies to thrive amidst the evolving AI landscape.

Economic Implications of AI

As artificial intelligence rapidly integrates into the fabric of the global economy, its economic implications are profound and far-reaching. Embedding AI technology into various sectors doesn't just promise increased efficiency; it challenges the conventional boundaries of industries. Its impact can be seen in the optimization of supply chains, enhancements in customer service, and even in redefining traditional roles within the workplace. However, alongside these opportunities are complexities and challenges that require careful navigation and strategic planning.

First and foremost, AI is reshaping the labor market. Automation driven by AI technologies threatens to replace certain manual and repetitive jobs, compelling the workforce to adapt to new realities. While AI could lead to job displacement in some areas, it simultaneously creates new opportunities in others. For instance, while manufacturing sectors might see a decline in assembly line positions, the demand for data scientists and AI specialists continues to grow. This shift necessitates a significant focus on retraining and education to equip workers with the skills necessary to thrive in an AI-driven economy.

The economic ramifications of AI extend into productivity and economic growth. AI technologies have the potential to drive significant productivity gains by automating routine tasks and processes, allowing human workers to focus on more complex and creative endeavors. This reallocation of labor resources can contribute to increased output and potentially higher GDP figures. However, the distribution of these gains can be uneven, posing a challenge to equality in economic benefits. Policymakers and business leaders alike must address these disparities to ensure inclusive economic growth.

For businesses, the integration of AI technologies is no longer optional but essential. Companies that successfully implement AI solutions can achieve a competitive edge through improved operational efficiencies and enhanced decision-making capabilities. AI's ability to analyze vast amounts of data quickly and accurately provides managers with insights that can inform strategic initiatives and uncover market opportunities that traditional methods might overlook. This shift necessitates a reevaluation of business models and the agility to adapt to a swiftly changing technological landscape.

Moreover, AI's impact is visible in the realm of financial markets. The advent of algorithms capable of executing trades at lightning speed is transforming trading floors worldwide. These algorithmic systems can detect patterns and execute transactions much faster than any human could, influencing asset prices and liquidity. As a result, financial institutions must develop new strategies to manage the risks and harness the opportunities these AI technologies present. Furthermore, regulators face the task of crafting policies that ensure fair practices and prevent systemic instability caused by these rapid technological advancements.

On a global scale, AI fosters international competitiveness. Countries that lead in AI research and application position themselves as leaders in the global economy. As nations race to capitalize on AI's potential, collaborations in AI development have become crucial. By fostering international partnerships, countries can share resources, research advancements, and regulatory practices, creating a comprehensive framework to maximize AI's benefits. These collaborations can lead to innovations that transcend national boundaries, driving global economic prosperity.

However, it is essential to consider the social contract as AI's influence continues to grow. The impact AI exerts on the global economy isn't solely about growth and efficiency. It also concerns how societies navigate ethical considerations and manage the displacement that AI-driven automation may cause. Building a sustainable economic environment necessitates balancing technological advancement with societal well-being. This balance requires governments, corporations, and individuals to collaborate in developing policies and frameworks that address ethical concerns and prioritize human-centric approaches to AI integration.

Yet, addressing these economic implications isn't just about managing the challenges AI presents. It's also about seizing the opportunities for transformative change. AI can act as a catalyst for pushing society toward innovative problem-solving methods, encouraging sectors to rethink their processes and prompting individuals to adopt lifelong learning as a norm. As we move forward, ensuring access to AI tools and education becomes vital to minimizing disparities and enabling equitable growth.

In summary, the economic implications of AI paint a complex picture, filled with challenges and opportunities. The potential for productivity increases and economic growth is substantial, yet these benefits must be managed thoughtfully to prevent exacerbating inequality. By fostering collaboration across sectors and borders, investing in skill development, and nurturing an ethos of ethical responsibility, society can steer the economic transformation AI promises towards a more inclusive and prosperous future. Embracing AI is not just about leveraging technology; it's about shaping an economy that reflects intelligence, adaptability, and humanity's enduring quest for progress.

International Collaboration in AI Advancements

As we delve deeper into the transformative power of artificial intelligence, the notion of international collaboration emerges as a cornerstone for AI advancements worldwide. In today's interconnected global economy, no single nation can claim superiority in AI development. Instead, a collaborative approach fosters innovation, sharing of knowledge, and distribution of technologies across borders. This collective effort is crucial to maximize AI's potential while addressing the varied challenges it presents.

By promoting international partnerships in AI development, countries can leverage diverse perspectives, leading to more comprehensive and inclusive AI systems. These partnerships enable the pooling of resources, which can accelerate research and development.

Given the exponential pace of AI evolution, collaboration becomes imperative to maintain a competitive edge and to ensure that progress doesn't become restricted by geographical or national boundaries.

Countries worldwide are increasingly recognizing the strategic importance of AI, striving to position themselves as leaders in this field. However, this competition doesn't preclude collaboration; in fact, it amplifies the need for it. Competitive nations can still benefit tremendously by partaking in joint research initiatives and sharing best practices. For example, the collaboration between China and the European Union highlights the potential for shared AI research goals, addressing everything from ethical considerations to technological breakthroughs.

Collaborative efforts often uncover unique opportunities for innovation that might remain unexplored within isolated national frameworks. Consider the partnerships between universities and research institutions across different countries which consistently produce significant AI developments. Through these alliances, researchers exchange data and insights, enhancing the overall quality and applicability of AI technologies. Such academic partnerships can also set global standards for AI ethics and safety, creating an international consensus that helps to address AI's ethical dilemmas.

International organizations play a pivotal role in facilitating these collaborations. Entities like the United Nations, the European Union, and the Organization for Economic Cooperation and Development have initiated programs to foster cross-border AI research and development. These organizations provide a platform for dialogue, policy-making, and consensus-building among countries, aligning them towards common goals such as ethical AI deployment, data privacy protection, and the equitable distribution of AI benefits.

The technological cooperation witnessed among nations extends beyond conventional software development. AI advancements in industries such as healthcare, transportation, and energy benefit significantly from global collaboration. For instance, international joint efforts in medical AI research can lead to breakthroughs in diagnostics and personalized treatments, applying insights gathered from diverse populations to create more effective healthcare solutions worldwide.

Moreover, collaborative AI projects often tackle global challenges like climate change, poverty, and pandemics. Sharing AI technologies and methodologies across countries enables a more effective response, as seen during the COVID-19 pandemic. By pooling resources and data, countries managed to use AI to develop vaccines, track virus spread, and optimize healthcare systems, demonstrating the power and necessity of international collaboration in crisis scenarios.

A crucial factor in fostering effective collaboration is establishing interoperability standards. Harmonizing technical protocols and data formats ensures that AI systems developed in various parts of the world can seamlessly interact and integrate. This interoperability is fundamental for cohesive development and deployment of AI technologies that span international borders without obstruction.

Cultural exchanges facilitated by collaboration also play a significant role in advancing AI. Understanding cultural contexts can lead to the development of AI systems that are more empathetic and considerate of different user needs. By incorporating diverse cultural insights, AI technologies can achieve a greater acceptance and wider applicability, reflecting the values and expectations of a global user base.

Nonetheless, international collaboration in AI isn't devoid of obstacles. Challenges such as regulatory discrepancies, data sovereignty issues, and geopolitical tensions can hinder cooperation. To overcome these barriers, countries need to engage in continual dialogue and negotiation, fostering trust and establishing aligned objectives. This requires diplomatic efforts and mutual willingness to accommodate differing national interests.

The future of AI hinges on our ability to foster international collaboration effectively. It's a future where countries aren't merely competing with each other but working side by side to forge new paths in AI that transcend borders. This cooperative model will not only drive technological advancement but also ensure that AI becomes a tool for global good, enhancing prosperity and well-being worldwide.

In conclusion, international partnerships in AI advancements are a testament to the potential power of global unity in the digital age. As AI continues to reshape the global economy, these collaborations have the capacity to foster a more equitable and progressive world, where technological innovation is intertwined with human values and shared achievements. When countries work together, the possibilities are limitless and the benefits are boundless, paving the way for a future that's enriched by the collective endeavor of all humanity.

Chapter 13:
Ensuring a Human-Centric AI Future

As we stand on the brink of an AI-dominated era, a steadfast commitment to ensuring a human-centric future is crucial. This commitment demands that AI systems not only enhance productivity and innovation but also align with core human values such as empathy, fairness, and dignity. Balancing the relentless advance of technology with the foundational principles of humanity involves integrating ethical frameworks directly into the development of AI. We must prioritize transparency and inclusivity at every level, ensuring algorithms are designed with a deep respect for human rights. By putting human values at the forefront, we resist the reduction of individuals to mere data points and champion a future where technology amplifies human potential rather than diminishes it. Such an approach will require vigilance, adaptability, and the collective resolve of innovators, leaders, and citizens alike. It's about crafting an AI trajectory that not only forecasts progress but also safeguards the ethical integrity of this progress, empowering us all to thrive in an AI-enhanced world.

Prioritizing Human Values

As we delve into the chapter on ensuring a human-centric AI future, the section "Prioritizing Human Values" stands out as a beacon, guiding our exploration into the essence of technology's role in our lives. The rise of artificial intelligence brings with it unparalleled potential, but also a responsibility to anchor its growth in the core values that define humanity. It's a pivotal time where technology and ethics must converge to chart a course for a future that enhances, rather than diminishes, our human experience.

In the rush to innovate and adopt AI solutions, it's easy to be swept away by the excitement of new capabilities and efficiencies. Yet, the crucial aspect often overlooked is how these advancements impact our fundamental human values. The true measure of progress isn't merely in the speed of technological adoption or the magnitude of economic growth; it's in how these innovations reflect and respect our collective principles.

What constitutes human values in the context of AI? The concept itself transcends cultural and regional boundaries, encompassing principles like fairness, transparency, privacy, and respect for individual autonomy. These values should underpin every stage of AI development and implementation. Fairness, for instance, demands that AI systems operate without bias, ensuring equal opportunity across demographics. Transparency is vital so individuals can understand and trust the systems influencing significant aspects of their lives.

Our world is more interconnected than ever, with technology acting as both the bridge and the barrier. While AI has the power to unify, it also risks deepening divides if not managed thoughtfully. Understanding and prioritizing human values in AI isn't just an ethical imperative; it's a social one. By crafting AI systems that echo and enhance our values, we avoid creating technologies that alienate or exclude large swathes of the population. This approach requires an inclusive mindset, considering diverse perspectives in AI development to fairly represent the intricacies of global society.

Privacy serves as another cornerstone of these values. In an AI-driven environment, personal data is the fuel powering countless decisions, from targeted advertising to healthcare interventions.

Protecting this data is paramount. Individuals must have confidence that their personal information won't be exploited or exposed without consent. This requires stringent policies and vigilant oversight to keep data security robust and breach-free.

Yet, the challenge lies not just in setting these values as goals, but in embedding them within the framework of AI systems. This calls for a collaborative approach, where technologists, ethicists, regulators, and the community jointly shape the rules governing AI usage. An ethical AI ecosystem thrives on collaboration. It involves defining best practices and standards that apply across varying contexts, ensuring that human dignity is upheld regardless of technological advancements.

Transparency also demands an active dialogue between developers and users. By demystifying the AI "black box," stakeholders can comprehend decision-making processes, leading to greater accountability. This knowledge empowerment enables users to have informed discussions about the potential risks and rewards, fostering a tech landscape where trust is as highly valued as innovation.

A crucial element in maintaining focus on human values is education. Supporting an informed populace through accessible AI literacy programs is a step toward empowering people to make choices that align with their ethical frameworks. This understanding, in turn, pressures corporations to align their AI strategies with public expectations. It creates a dynamic where educated users demand more ethical practices, pushing the industry toward more responsible innovations.

Leadership is another pivotal factor when prioritizing human values within AI development. Business leaders and policymakers play a vital role by setting ethical benchmarks and striving to meet them consistently. Their commitment to ethical practices influences organizational culture, driving a trickle-down effect that permeates every level of AI usage and development.

The journey toward a human-centric future is one where ongoing vigilance is necessary. The pace of AI development will only quicken, presenting new challenges for integrating human values with emerging capabilities. As innovators, advocates, and everyday users, staying attuned to these developments ensures we hold technology accountable to the values we cherish.

Human values should not be treated as static; they're dynamic, evolving alongside society. As such, the frameworks and policies designed to protect these values must remain agile, adapting to new challenges and opportunities. By creating adaptable models that are regularly reviewed and updated, we can ensure AI systems consistently align with contemporary ethical standards.

This isn't a simple task, nor one that can be achieved overnight. It takes deliberate actions and steadfast resolve. The beauty of this endeavor, however, lies in its potential to transform AI into a force that complements human abilities and advances society in meaningful ways. The integration of human values into AI is not merely philosophical rhetoric; it is a practical guide for building technologies that uplift humanity as a whole.

In conclusion, prioritizing human values in the age of AI is about more than ethics; it's about envisioning a future where technology and humanity coexist synergistically. As architects of this future, we must champion a vision of AI that's inextricably intertwined with the values that define us. This alignment not only safeguards our societal principles but also crafts a world where both humans and machines thrive in harmony, setting the stage for a future that we can all embrace.

Safeguarding Human Rights

Amid the rapid ascent of artificial intelligence, the pressing need to safeguard human rights becomes increasingly paramount. AI, with its unparalleled capacity for analysis and automation, holds the potential to redefine societal structures. But as with any powerful tool, it poses both immense opportunities and profound risks. The challenge lies in harnessing AI's capabilities while staunchly defending the rights and freedoms that are fundamental to human dignity. This endeavor requires vigilance, action, and a steadfast commitment to integrating ethical principles into every corner of AI development and deployment.

At the heart of safeguarding human rights in an AI-driven world is ensuring the privacy and autonomy of individuals. The ability of AI systems to analyze vast datasets redefines what is possible, but it also amplifies concerns about surveillance and misuse of personal information. Striking a balance between leveraging data for progress and maintaining individual privacy is crucial. This balance is not just a technical challenge but a moral imperative, requiring collaboration between technologists, policymakers, and civil society.

Freedom from discrimination is another cornerstone of human rights that demands protection in the age of AI. As AI systems are deployed in areas ranging from employment to law enforcement, the potential for bias in algorithms can lead to unjust outcomes. Ensuring AI systems are transparent and rigorously tested for fairness is essential. Rigorous benchmarking and consistent evaluation of AI applications must be prioritized to prevent the automation of existing societal biases.

Moreover, AI's ability to influence public opinion through information dissemination warrants caution and regulation. With algorithms curating content on social media platforms and search engines, the integrity of information is at stake. Protecting the right to access accurate information requires vigilance against algorithmic manipulation and the propagation of misinformation. It calls for AI algorithms to be designed with accountability in mind, guaranteeing that truthfulness and transparency are upheld.

Ensuring access to justice in an AI-enabled society is an evolving challenge. As AI begins to play a role in decision-making processes traditionally governed by human oversight, particularly in legal or administrative scenarios, it is vital to guarantee that these systems do not erode access to fair representation. Safeguards must be instituted to ensure AI-enhanced processes are transparent and include mechanisms for appeal and review, upholding the principles of due process.

Another vital facet is ensuring equitable access to AI technology itself. Unequal distribution of AI capabilities risks widening existing societal gaps. The democratization of AI, in terms of access to its tools and benefits, is a human rights issue. Ensuring that marginalized communities are not left behind in the technological revolution requires intentional policies and initiatives aimed at fostering inclusivity and equitable participation.

Educational systems must be adapted to equip future generations with the skills and awareness necessary to navigate an AI-pervasive world. As AI reshapes job markets and societal norms, education systems have a responsibility to prepare individuals not only to coexist with AI but also to question and influence the ethical frameworks within which AI operates. This preparation is essential to fostering a society that both benefits from AI innovations and remains vigilant in the protection of human rights.

The role of international collaboration cannot be understated in the quest to protect human rights in an AI era. AI is a global phenomenon, transcending national borders and regulatory environments. As such, the establishment of international norms and agreements is critical. Collaborative efforts can help to standardize best practices across industries and regions, ensuring that the protection of human rights is universally recognized as a benchmark of AI development and deployment.

Industries and corporations have a pivotal role in this safeguarding mission. By adopting corporate social responsibility practices that prioritize human rights, businesses can lead by example. Incorporating ethical AI guidelines into corporate strategies sets a precedent and encourages the development of technologies that respect and promote human rights. Such initiatives create a ripple effect, prompting others in the industry to follow suit.

The journey towards a human-centric AI future, where technological innovation is aligned with the broader goal of safeguarding human rights, is complex and requires commitment from all sectors of society. It demands a multifaceted approach, involving technological solutions, regulatory frameworks, and a shared societal ethos that prioritizes human dignity above all. By fostering a collaborative environment where various stakeholders engage in ongoing dialogue and action, we can ensure that AI serves as a force for good, enhancing the human condition and upholding the values we hold dear.

Chapter 14:
Legal and Regulatory Considerations

As artificial intelligence becomes a pivotal force in modern workplaces, navigating the legal and regulatory landscape is no longer optional—it's essential. Business leaders, technologists, and policymakers find themselves at a crossroads, balancing innovation with responsibility. Crafting regulations that are adaptable yet robust requires a forward-thinking approach, aligning with the dynamic nature of AI. Complying with frameworks designed to ensure transparency and protect rights can foster trust and spur innovation. Companies must stay informed about legislative developments while being proactive in adopting compliance strategies. The challenge lies in harmonizing diverse global regulations to create a coherent strategy that encourages ethical AI development, stimulating growth without compromising core values. By understanding these complexities and embracing regulatory rigor, organizations not only mitigate risks but also pave the way for sustainable advancement in the AI-driven era.

Navigating AI Legislation

As artificial intelligence (AI) continues to reshape industries and redefine the future of work, the legal landscape is also undergoing rapid transformation. Navigating AI legislation requires an in-depth understanding of evolving rules and policies being enacted worldwide. With governments grappling with the challenges and promises of AI, businesses face a complex web of regulations that demand diligence and adaptability. These regulations aim to balance innovation with ethical considerations, ensuring AI systems are transparent, fair, and non-discriminatory.

One of the foremost considerations when navigating AI legislation is data privacy. As data becomes the lifeblood of AI systems, the protection of personal information has emerged as a pivotal issue. Laws like the European Union's General Data Protection Regulation (GDPR) have set stringent standards on data handling and user consent, influencing global policies and operational practices. Companies must align their AI strategies with these regulations to safeguard individual privacy, avoid substantial penalties, and maintain consumer trust.

The challenge for organizations is not just about compliance; it is about embracing the spirit of these regulations to foster an ethical AI ecosystem. This involves re-evaluating data collection methodologies, implementing advanced security measures, and establishing clear data usage protocols. By doing so, businesses can both comply with the current regulatory landscape and anticipate future legislative shifts, positioning themselves as leaders in ethical AI deployment.

Equally vital is understanding the implications of AI legislation on algorithmic accountability and transparency. Governments increasingly pressure companies to ensure AI systems operate without perpetuating biases or discriminatory practices. Laws are emerging that require documentation of AI decision-making processes, enabling stakeholders to scrutinize and challenge the outcomes. For businesses, this means embedding transparency into the core of AI development, offering explanations for AI-driven decisions, and continuously auditing algorithms to prevent bias.

Algorithmic bias presents a profound challenge that AI legislation seeks to address. Machine learning models, when trained on biased data, can replicate and even amplify existing prejudices, leading to unfair outcomes. Legislation around the world is beginning to target these issues, pushing for fairness and accountability in AI systems. For companies, it's imperative to develop robust frameworks for identifying and mitigating bias, using diverse data sets and involving multidisciplinary teams in model development.

As AI technologies evolve, so too do the ethical questions surrounding their use, leading to varying legislative approaches globally. Some countries prioritize innovation and economic competitiveness, adopting a more permissive regulatory environment, while others focus heavily on ethical considerations and societal impact. For global companies, this variance requires a flexible approach to AI integration, tailoring their operations to the legal landscapes of each region they operate in.

In the United States, AI legislation is more fragmented, with individual states introducing their own laws alongside federal guidelines. For instance, the California Consumer Privacy Act (CCPA) offers a regulatory framework that shares similarities with the GDPR, albeit with distinctions that require careful navigation by businesses operating in the state. Meanwhile, other states and federal bodies continue to develop specific AI regulations, emphasizing the need for businesses to stay attuned to legislative developments.

Conversely, in Asia, countries like China are leading with proactive government-led AI initiatives, aiming to establish dominance in AI technology and ethical standards globally. China's approach emphasizes developing AI capabilities while concurrently creating a regulatory framework that fosters controlled and responsible use. This illustrates different state priorities and strategies, compelling international firms to continuously adapt their operations and compliance strategies.

The global nature of AI legislation necessitates international collaboration and knowledge exchange between regulators, industry leaders, and academia. Multinational organizations must actively engage in dialogues with policymakers, contributing to the development of practical and forward-looking AI governance frameworks. By participating in international forums and discussions, companies can help shape the regulatory environment in ways that promote both innovation and public trust.

As we look to the future, the legal terrain of AI will likely become even more intricate with advancements in AI technologies. Emerging fields such as autonomous systems, deepfake technologies, and AI-generated content bring new regulatory challenges that require progressive solutions. Businesses must remain vigilant, expecting and preparing for new legal norms that will inevitably surface as technology continues to evolve.

Education and awareness also play crucial roles in navigating AI legislation. Organizations must ensure their teams are well-versed in relevant laws, fostering a culture of compliance and ethical responsibility. This involves continuous professional development, cross-disciplinary training, and recruitment of legal experts specializing in AI-related issues. Investing in legal and ethical expertise will not only ensure compliance but also enable businesses to leverage AI more strategically and innovatively.

In closing, navigating AI legislation is as much about compliance as it is about seizing the opportunity to lead in ethical AI practices. Organizations equipped to adapt to and anticipate regulatory changes will not only minimize risks but will also enhance their reputation as trustworthy, forward-thinking enterprises. Through strategic planning, proactive engagement with policy developments, and an unwavering commitment to ethical responsibility, businesses can thrive in the dynamically evolving AI-driven world.

Ensuring Compliance and Transparency

In an era where artificial intelligence is reshaping industries and redefining work paradigms, ensuring compliance and transparency isn't just a legal obligation—it's a cornerstone for fostering trust and stability in the AI-driven workplace. As AI becomes more ingrained into business processes, the necessity to operate within legal frameworks while maintaining open practices is paramount. Companies that prioritize these aspects are not only protecting themselves from potential legal pitfalls but are also positioning themselves as leaders in ethical innovation.

Compliance in the context of AI revolves around adhering to regulations that govern data privacy, ethical AI deployment, and operational accountability. The regulatory landscape is rapidly evolving, with new laws and guidelines continuously emerging as governments and international bodies attempt to address the complexities introduced by AI. For example, the European Union's General Data Protection Regulation (GDPR) sets a high bar for data protection and has influenced similar legislation globally. Organizations must stay abreast of such regulations to navigate legal requirements effectively, preventing costly breaches that can arise from non-compliance.

But compliance isn't merely about avoiding penalties; it's about cultivating an environment where AI systems are used responsibly and ethically. This involves a comprehensive understanding of the algorithms at play and the potential consequences of their deployment. Businesses should implement robust governance frameworks that include oversight mechanisms to monitor AI's impact on decision-making processes. By doing so, they safeguard against unintended biases and ensure that AI-driven outcomes align with organizational values and societal norms.

Transparency plays an equally critical role in nurturing trust among stakeholders, including employees, customers, and regulatory bodies. Achieving transparency, however, can be a daunting task given the "black box" nature of many AI models. It's important for companies to demystify these systems, providing clear explanations of how data is used and decisions are made. Transparency fosters an atmosphere of honesty and accountability, which can empower consumers and safeguard against the erosion of trust.

One approach to enhancing transparency is to adopt explainable AI (XAI) techniques. These methods aim to make AI systems more interpretable, enabling stakeholders to understand the logic and reasoning behind AI-driven decisions. By making AI processes more interpretable, organizations can not only build trust but also facilitate audits and compliance checks, ensuring adherence to legal and ethical standards.

Moreover, involving diverse teams in the AI development process can further promote transparency and ethical compliance. Various perspectives encourage a more comprehensive evaluation of AI systems and mitigate the risks of cognitive biases. This diversity ensures that AI applications are not only technically sound but also socially responsible. Encouraging cross-disciplinary collaboration enhances the robustness of AI systems and aligns them more closely with human-centric values.

Organizations should also focus on establishing clear lines of communication when it comes to AI capabilities and limitations. This involves training employees, informing customers, and cooperating with regulators to ensure a shared understanding. Comprehensive education and communication strategies can bridge knowledge gaps, dispelling misconceptions and reinforcing confidence in AI technologies.

In addition, fostering a culture of transparency and compliance requires continuous evaluation and adaptation. Companies must be agile in their approach, reviewing policies and practices regularly to respond to new developments in AI technologies and regulatory changes. Proactive adaptation is key to maintaining compliance, as static policies can quickly become outdated in the face of rapid technological advancements.

Accountability is another critical component of ensuring compliance and transparency. It calls for identifying responsibility across the organizational hierarchy, ensuring that all stakeholders—from developers to C-suite executives—are committed to upholding ethical standards. Establishing accountability frameworks can help delineate roles and responsibilities, as well as foster a culture of integrity throughout the organization.

The integration of AI into the workplace continues to redefine our understanding of compliance and transparency. Organizations that skillfully navigate these complexities are better equipped to maintain ethical standards while achieving their strategic goals. They recognize that regulation isn't a barrier but a guide towards sustainable growth and innovation.

Ultimately, a proactive approach to compliance and transparency goes beyond mitigating risks; it's about aligning AI systems with human values and ensuring that these technologies serve the greater good. A commitment to ethical AI practices will not only protect businesses from legal repercussions but also strengthen their reputation as trustworthy and responsible actors in an increasingly AI-centric world. In doing so, they lay the groundwork for a future where AI not only enhances productivity but also enriches human life, fostering an inclusive and equitable society for all.

Chapter 15:
AI-Driven Customer Experience

The rapid integration of AI into customer interactions is transforming how businesses understand and satisfy consumer needs, enhancing the customer experience like never before. By leveraging advanced data analytics and machine learning algorithms, companies can deliver personalized experiences that align closely with individual preferences and behaviors. This shift not only supports deeper customer insights but also fosters stronger relationships built on trust and transparency. The potential for AI to predict customer needs and tailor interactions in real-time offers a competitive advantage in a crowded marketplace. Companies investing in AI-driven strategies are finding that these innovations not only enhance satisfaction but also contribute to long-term loyalty and advocacy. As businesses continue to harness AI's capabilities, they must maintain a balance between automation and the human touch, ensuring technology enhances rather than replaces the personal connections that remain pivotal in customer relations. Embracing AI-driven customer experiences requires visionary leadership and a commitment to the ethical implementation of these powerful tools, setting the stage for lasting customer engagement in an ever-evolving digital era.

Personalization and Customer Insights

In today's AI-driven landscape, the concept of customer experience is undergoing a fundamental transformation. At the heart of this evolution lies personalization and the nuanced insights that AI can unravel from vast troves of customer data. As businesses strive to stand out in a competitive market, understanding the individual needs and preferences of their customers has become more crucial than ever. This is where AI steps in, offering unprecedented opportunities to tailor experiences to the unique expectations of every consumer.

AI technologies, such as machine learning and deep learning, empower companies to analyze customer behavior, preferences, and interactions at a depth that was previously unimaginable. By sifting through data from multiple sources—ranging from purchase history and browsing behavior to social media interactions—AI systems can identify patterns and predict future behaviors. This capability is invaluable for businesses seeking to move beyond a one-size-fits-all strategy and instead offer bespoke experiences that resonate with individual customers on a personal level.

Personalization driven by AI is not limited to product recommendations or customized marketing messages. It extends into every touchpoint of the customer journey. From dynamic pricing and tailored promotions to personalized customer service interactions, AI can adjust these elements in real-time, providing a seamless and adaptive experience. The impact of such tailored interactions leads to increased customer satisfaction, loyalty, and ultimately, higher conversion rates.

Consider the retail industry, where AI-powered insights have redefined how businesses understand their customers. By leveraging data analytics, retailers can predict trends, optimize inventory, and personalize in-store experiences. For instance, AI can analyze foot traffic and purchasing patterns to inform merchandising decisions or suggest personalized product selections based on past behaviors. This level of personalization enhances the shopping experience by making it more relevant and enjoyable for customers.

In the financial services sector, AI-driven personalization plays an equally transformative role. Financial institutions can leverage AI to offer personalized portfolio recommendations, tailored financial advice, and fraud detection strategies based on a client's specific financial habits and life circumstances. This creates a more personalized relationship with customers, fostering trust and positioning institutions as more than just service providers, but as partners in their financial journeys.

A crucial aspect of this personalization is the delivery of customer insights. AI systems don't just compile data; they translate it into actionable insights that can inform strategic decisions. By visualizing customer journeys and understanding touchpoints, businesses can identify opportunities for improvement and innovation. These insights provide a clearer picture of customer satisfaction levels and areas where service delivery can be enhanced, driving continuous improvement and innovation.

Moreover, AI-enabled platforms allow businesses to experiment with different variables and scenarios to see how changes might impact customer experience. This predictive modeling lets companies anticipate needs and preferences, enabling proactive engagement rather than reactive responses. It transforms how businesses approach customer relationship management, shifting the focus from simply meeting needs to predicting and exceeding expectations.

The power of AI in personalization doesn't just change individual interactions but influences overall business strategies. By understanding customer segments on a granular level, businesses can tailor their products, services, and marketing strategies to align with customer expectations. This targeted approach can result in more efficient allocation of resources and higher return on investment.

However, the journey to personalization and actionable insights comes with its challenges. One significant concern is data privacy. As

AI systems collect and analyze vast amounts of personal data, businesses must navigate the fine line between personalization and privacy. It is imperative for companies to ensure that they adhere to stringent data protection regulations and foster a culture of trust with their customers. Transparency about data usage and robust security measures are essential components in maintaining customer trust.

Another challenge lies in the integration of AI into existing business systems. For AI to be effective, businesses must ensure their data is clean, accurate, and comprehensive. This might involve upgrading legacy systems or investing in new digital infrastructure. The complexity of such an overhaul requires careful planning and execution.

Furthermore, businesses must invest in training and upskilling their workforce to effectively leverage AI technologies. Teams need to be equipped with both the technical skills to manage AI tools and the critical thinking skills to interpret data insights. Empowered with the right knowledge, teams can maximize the potential of AI in enhancing customer experience and driving business outcomes.

Despite these challenges, the potential of AI in personalization and customer insights remains profound. As AI technology continues to evolve, its ability to understand and predict customer needs will only become more sophisticated. Businesses that embrace these capabilities stand to gain a significant competitive advantage, positioning themselves as leaders in customer experience.

Ultimately, the integration of AI into personalization strategies isn't just about technology—it's about creating meaningful connections with customers. It requires a balance between innovation and ethics, ensuring that as businesses deliver more personalized experiences, they do so with respect for individual privacy and societal values. This balance will define the future of customer relationships in an AI-driven world.

Building Customer Trust with AI

In the ever-evolving landscape of business strategies, building customer trust is a cornerstone for sustainable success. As companies increasingly adopt AI-driven approaches to enhance customer experience, striking the right balance between innovation and trust becomes paramount. The integration of artificial intelligence into customer interfaces offers unprecedented opportunities to personalize interactions and derive deeper insights, but it also raises concerns about data security, transparency, and ethical considerations.

Trust is not bestowed but earned, and in the realm of AI, that's even more critical. Customers must feel confident that their personal information is safe and used ethically. To establish this, businesses must prioritize transparency, clearly communicating how AI technologies are utilized to serve their needs. One practical approach is to create user-friendly privacy policies and data use agreements that are both comprehensive and understandable. This proactive disclosure isn't just about legal compliance; it's about cultivating genuine customer confidence.

AI architectures are complex, and customers might be skeptical about algorithms making decisions on their behalf. To mitigate this, companies should adopt explainable AI (XAI) frameworks. These frameworks ensure decisions are not black-box processes but are instead understandable and justifiable. For example, when a recommendation engine suggests a product, a brief explanation or insights into the decision process can demystify AI operations and build trust. Empowering customers with the 'why' behind AI's actions transforms ambiguity into assurance.

Beyond transparency and explanation lies the ethical dimension of AI, which is increasingly important to conscientious consumers. Implementing an ethical framework for AI use involves defining what the company stands for and how its values are integrated into AI processes. Companies need to ensure that AI applications are free from biases that can lead to unfair customer experiences. Regular audits and ethical reviews should be part of the AI lifecycle to uphold accountability and fairness.

The robustness of AI systems in safeguarding personal data also plays a crucial role in trust. With growing concerns about data breaches, companies must implement state-of-the-art security measures. Encryption, anonymization, and regular vulnerability assessments can reinforce data protection. Additionally, businesses should establish a quick and effective response strategy to manage any potential data breaches, communicating transparently with customers if incidents occur. This proactive approach not only minimizes damage but can strengthen trust by demonstrating a commitment to customer security.

On the flip side, AI offers incredible capabilities for personalization, which when used rightly, can enhance trust. By harnessing machine learning, businesses can deliver personalized experiences that resonate with individual customers. Understanding preferences, predicting needs, and personalizing communications creates a sense of relevance and engagement. However, personalization must be balanced with privacy, respecting the customer's comfort levels and preferences on data usage, ensuring the personalization feels like an enhancement rather than an intrusion.

Moreover, cultivating a customer-centric culture within the organization is essential for trust-building. AI tools should complement this by providing employees with insights and solutions that empower them to offer superior service. When staff are well-informed and AI-enhanced, they can anticipate customer needs, address concerns swiftly, and elevate the overall experience. Each positive interaction nurtures trust, showing customers they are valued and understood in a world where digital often feels impersonal.

A collaborative approach can add another layer of trust. Encouraging customer feedback on AI-driven processes involves them in shaping their experience, signaling that their opinions are valued. By tailoring AI applications based on this feedback, businesses not only improve their services but also reinforce the notion that the customer is central to their innovations.

Continuous monitoring and adaptation are vital as AI systems evolve. Adaptability ensures that AI implementations remain compliant with the changing regulatory landscape and aligned with customer expectations. Incorporating customer trust metrics into AI performance assessments allows businesses to track and respond to shifts in customer sentiment, making timely adjustments to policies or technologies when needed.

Finally, consistent and open communication plays a significant role in customer trust. Businesses should regularly update customers on AI advancements, changes in data policies, or new features resulting from AI implementation. Newsletters, blogs, or direct correspondence can keep customers informed, reducing suspicion and fostering an atmosphere of inclusion in the digital journey.

In conclusion, AI presents a dual conduit—one for advancing customer experience and the other for reinforcing trust. To achieve both, a business must be transparent, ethical, and responsive, integrating AI into its core ethos while being mindful of its broad impacts on customers. By building a foundation of trust, companies can not only leverage AI for innovation but also create lasting relationships that transcend technological fluctuations and market changes, driving success in a digitally native future.

Chapter 16:
Automating Routine Tasks

Stepping into the realm of automating routine tasks, we delve into how AI is revolutionizing efficiency in the modern workplace. Mundane and repetitive responsibilities, once absorbing significant human effort, are now deftly handled by intelligent systems, freeing up invaluable resources for creative and strategic pursuits. This transformation is not merely about replacing human roles but augmenting them, allowing professionals to focus on higher-level problem-solving and innovation. Automation enhances precision and reliability, reducing the margin for error in routine operations. However, the key challenge lies in judiciously balancing automation with human input, ensuring that the human touch remains integral where empathy and nuanced judgment are paramount. The journey is neither straightforward nor without its hurdles, but harnessing automation holds unparalleled potential to elevate productivity and satisfaction, reshaping the workplace landscape for today's professionals and tomorrow's innovators.

Efficiency Through Automation

Automation is no longer science fiction. It has crossed the chasm from a futuristic concept to a practical business strategy that's reshaping modern workplaces. At its core, automation leverages technology to perform tasks that once required manual effort, freeing up human resources to focus on more complex and value-driven activities.

Automation's potential isn't just about cutting costs or doing things faster—it's about transforming how organizations operate and innovate.

Imagine the mundane tasks that fill up a typical workday: scheduling meetings, processing invoices, managing email correspondence—the list goes on. While essential, these routine tasks consume significant time and attention that could otherwise be directed toward strategic thinking and innovation. Automating these processes not only increases efficiency but also reduces errors and allows employees to engage in more meaningful work.

Businesses have begun to harness the power of automation in various facets, from streamlining operational workflows to enhancing customer experiences. The deployment of AI-driven software can now handle repetitive tasks with consistent accuracy. For example, in finance, robotic process automation (RPA) tools can reconcile accounts and process claims with minimal human intervention. Such systems often work tirelessly around the clock, providing a level of operational consistency that's challenging to achieve manually.

The notion of automation-enabled efficiency might spark concern among the workforce about job displacement. However, history tells us a different story. The introduction of new technologies often leads to the evolution of job roles rather than their extinction. As routine tasks become automated, there's a growing demand for skills that are inherently human—creativity, emotional intelligence, complex problem-solving, and strategic planning. Thus, automation doesn't just replace jobs but reshapes them, opening new avenues for career development.

Industries across the spectrum are demonstrating how automation can drive business efficiency. In manufacturing, automated robots on assembly lines have sped up production and minimized defects. In customer service, chatbots equipped with natural language processing

(NLP) can handle customer inquiries, providing quick responses and solutions. These applications enhance service delivery and allow human agents to manage more intricate customer issues.

Despite the clear advantages, successful automation requires a strategic approach. It's imperative for organizations to identify which processes are ripe for automation and which ones still need the nuanced touch of human input. Thoughtful prioritization can lead to maximum efficiency without sacrificing quality. This balance ensures that automation serves as a tool to enhance human capability rather than diminish it.

Implementing automation isn't just a technical challenge; it requires cultural change within an organization. Employees need to embrace new ways of working and develop trust in automated systems. This transition can be facilitated by involving staff in the process, offering training, and highlighting how automation can enhance their roles. When employees understand that automation is there to augment their work—not replace them—they're more likely to support its deployment.

Moreover, the cost of automation, while significant, should be viewed as an investment rather than an expense. Companies are finding that the return on such investments often manifests not only in operational savings but also in improved competitiveness and the capacity for innovation. In rapidly changing markets, the agility provided by automation can be a critical differentiator.

Organizations must also consider the ethical implications of automation. Ensuring that automated systems operate transparently and ethically should be a top priority. Proper oversight and regulation are essential to prevent biases in automated decision-making processes, ensuring equitable outcomes for all stakeholders.

As technology continues to evolve at a breakneck pace, the potential for automation will only grow in scope and sophistication. Businesses that are willing to embrace this change stand to gain a significant competitive edge. By understanding that automation is not merely an efficiency tool but a catalyst for innovation and transformation, companies can craft more resilient and forward-thinking operational strategies.

In conclusion, the journey towards efficiency through automation revolves around leveraging technology smartly while keeping human potential at the forefront. As we move forward, the collaboration between humans and machines will unlock unprecedented opportunities, pushing the boundaries of what we thought was possible in the workplace. Automation isn't an end—it's a means to achieving a more productive and innovative future.

Balancing Automation and Human Input

As the world eagerly embraces AI, the allure of automating routine tasks grows irresistible. In the whirlwind of technological advancement, businesses find themselves on a tightrope, striving to balance automation with the invaluable touch of human input. This balance is essential, as it shapes efficiency, creativity, and job satisfaction. The allure of complete automation is often tempered by the understanding that human intuition and creativity remain indispensable.

Routine tasks are ripe for automation. These are the repetitive, time-consuming activities that machines can handle with remarkable precision and efficiency. Automated systems can seamlessly manage tasks such as data entry, invoice processing, and inventory tracking. Such systems don't tire or err, making them perfect for jobs that require consistency and accuracy. Automation, therefore, promises not only increased productivity but also the liberation of employees from mundane tasks, allowing them to focus on more meaningful work.

However, the human aspect cannot be sidelined. Humans bring creativity, emotional intelligence, and problem-solving capabilities that machines cannot replicate. Consider customer service, where understanding and empathy are vital. While chatbots and automated systems can handle basic inquiries, complex issues often require a human touch. This calls for a hybrid approach, where routine tasks are automated to free up humans for interactions that need a personal connection.

This interplay between automation and human input is not just practical. It's strategic. Companies are discovering that their workforce, enhanced by AI, can drive significant innovation and customer satisfaction. By allocating mundane tasks to machines, individuals can cultivate skills in areas that truly matter, such as critical thinking, innovation, and relationship management. Thus, automation should be seen as a tool that enhances human capacity, not replaces it.

Designing a balanced approach requires understanding specific organizational needs. Companies should first identify which tasks can be automated without compromising quality or human input. These decisions should be guided by an assessment of how automation can complement human strengths. It's not about replacing humans; it's about positioning them where they can add the most value.

Moreover, feedback loops between humans and machines can improve systems over time. When human insights are fed back into automated processes, the system evolves, becoming more efficient and effective. This feedback loop fosters continuous improvement, enabling systems to adapt and meet changing needs.

Training and development play a pivotal role in this balancing act. As automation takes over routine tasks, businesses must invest in upskilling their employees. The workforce should be adept not only at managing and maintaining AI systems but also at leveraging these technologies to innovate and solve complex problems. This shift demands an ongoing commitment to learning, where adaptability becomes a key competency.

It's important to acknowledge the concerns around job displacement due to automation. While there's a risk, history shows that technology also creates new roles and opportunities. The challenge for businesses is to facilitate this transition, ensuring that their employees are ready for new roles that emerge. This reskilling can turn perceived threats into opportunities for growth and advancement, aligning workforce capabilities with strategic goals.

Culture plays a critical role too. Organizations must foster a culture that embraces technology while valuing the human contribution. This dual focus ensures that technology serves the organization and its people rather than becoming a driving force that dictates direction. Inclusive decision-making processes invite diverse perspectives, leading to more balanced outcomes that consider both technological capabilities and human needs.

Ultimately, the equilibrium between automation and human input is about choice. It's about choosing where automation can enhance operations and where it would detract from the human touch that defines customer relationships and innovative progress. This choice reflects an organization's identity and values, impacting how it interacts with clients and the broader community.

As businesses navigate this landscape, it helps to remain focused on long-term goals rather than short-term gains. The effective integration of automation involves strategic foresight and a commitment to cultural evolution. By embracing automation as a partner, companies can harness its strengths while elevating human input, creating a harmonious environment where both can thrive.

Chapter 17:
AI in Talent Acquisition and Management

In today's rapidly evolving job market, AI is revolutionizing how companies attract, retain, and develop their workforce. By leveraging sophisticated AI tools, recruitment processes have become faster, more efficient, and data-driven, enabling recruiters to identify top talent with precision and reduced bias. AI-powered analytics offer unprecedented insights into employee performance and potential, paving the way for tailored development plans that align individual aspirations with organizational goals. These technologies facilitate a deeper understanding of employee engagement, allowing companies to foster a more dynamic and supportive work environment. As AI continues to permeate talent management, leaders are encouraged to harness its potential thoughtfully, ensuring that the human essence remains at the heart of their strategic initiatives. With AI as a partner, businesses can unlock new levels of innovation and adaptability, positioning themselves for sustainable growth and success in the modern workforce.

AI Tools for Recruitment

The landscape of talent acquisition is undergoing a remarkable transformation as artificial intelligence (AI) takes center stage in recruitment processes worldwide. Organizations striving to stay ahead in the competitive business environment are increasingly leveraging

AI-driven tools to streamline their hiring processes, minimize biases, and identify top talent with unprecedented speed and accuracy. These tools are not only reshaping the recruitment field but also challenging the traditional methods that have long been a staple in human resources.

One significant advantage that AI tools bring to recruitment is their ability to manage large volumes of candidate data effortlessly. With the influx of applications for any given role, sifting through resumes manually can be both time-consuming and error-prone. AI systems can quickly analyze thousands of applications, identifying candidates whose qualifications and experiences align closely with the job specifications. This efficiency doesn't just save companies time and resources, it also enables HR professionals to focus their efforts on more strategic aspects of recruitment.

Moreover, AI-driven recruitment platforms harness the power of machine learning algorithms to improve over time. These platforms learn from past hiring successes and failures, continuously refining their criteria and recommendations. The iterative process enhances the precision of candidate selection, ensuring that the individuals being considered meet not only the explicit requirements but also align with the company's culture and values. Such AI systems provide a personalized candidate experience aimed at attracting those most likely to thrive within the organization's ecosystem.

AI tools are also transforming the initial stages of candidate interaction, especially through the use of chatbots and virtual recruiting assistants. These AI-powered assistants can engage with candidates in real-time, answering queries, providing feedback, and gathering necessary information to progress the recruitment cycle. By offering candidates prompt responses and information, AI tools play a vital role in enhancing the candidate experience, bolstering a company's reputation as a forward-thinking, applicant-friendly organization.

Despite the substantial advancements AI tools bring to recruitment, they are not without their challenges and pitfalls. A primary concern is ensuring that the algorithms that drive these tools are free from biases that could skew hiring outcomes. As AI systems learn from historical data, there's a risk of perpetuating biases present in past hiring decisions. Thus, the implementation of fairness frameworks and routine audits of AI-driven recruitment tools are essential steps in fostering a diverse and inclusive workplace.

The predictive capabilities of AI tools also extend into analyzing market trends and labor demographics. By evaluating the supply and demand of specific skill sets, businesses can make informed decisions about recruitment strategies and workforce planning. This predictive analysis allows recruiters to adjust their approaches proactively, rather than reacting to shifts in the job market as they occur. Such strategic foresight can be crucial in industries where the technology landscape—and the skills required to navigate it—evolves rapidly.

AI tools are harnessing the potential of natural language processing (NLP) to perform tasks previously thought to require a human touch. For instance, sentiment analysis in employer reviews or social media posts provides insights into potential red flags regarding candidates' reputations or attitudes. NLP tools can evaluate the language used in interviews or correspondence to gauge candidates' soft skills, such as communication and empathy, which are vital in many roles. The nuance captured by NLP provides a more holistic view of a candidate's capabilities beyond mere technical skills.

The integration of AI into recruitment doesn't signal the obsolescence of human recruiters; rather, it redefines their role. Recruiters armed with AI tools can shift their focus from administrative tasks to strategic activities, such as relationship building, candidate engagement, and employer branding. Emotional intelligence, negotiation skills, and deep industry knowledge remain irreplaceable skills that AI can't replicate, thus emphasizing the human-AI synergy in recruitment.

In conclusion, AI tools stand as a transformative force in the talent acquisition arena. They offer unparalleled efficiency, accuracy, and strategic insight, reshaping how organizations attract and secure top-tier talent. However, the journey towards seamless integration of these tools requires vigilant attention to ethical considerations and a commitment to maintaining a human-centric recruitment experience. As AI continues to evolve, so too will its impact on the recruitment industry, driving future innovations and setting new standards for excellence in talent acquisition.

Employee Development with AI Support

In the swiftly evolving landscape of AI-driven workplaces, nurturing employee development becomes both a challenge and an opportunity. It's no secret that AI tools and platforms are reshaping how we view professional growth, and they're doing so in a way that's unprecedented. By personalizing learning experiences and offering real-time feedback, AI-supported development systems are empowering employees like never before. The integration of AI into employee development is carving a new path, one that harmonizes technology with human potential, creating a symbiotic relationship that fuels unprecedented growth.

AI can tailor learning pathways for employees based on their individual strengths, weaknesses, and career aspirations. Traditional training programs often operate under a one-size-fits-all approach, which can stunt individual progress. However, AI-driven platforms, using analytics and machine learning, analyze an employee's performance data and learning style to curate a bespoke development plan. This personalized approach ensures that learning is not only continuous but also engaging and relevant. Employees are more likely to be motivated when they see a direct link between their efforts and personal growth targets.

Moreover, AI facilitates an environment of proactive learning by predicting skill gaps and future needs. By examining industry trends, organizational objectives, and global skill demands, AI systems can anticipate the skills that will be critical in the coming years. This foresight allows companies to prepare their workforce for future challenges, fostering a culture of adaptability and resilience. The concept of lifelong learning is no longer an ideal; it's a necessity. Employees who engage in continuous learning are not only more productive but also more innovative, contributing significantly to a company's competitive edge.

The role of AI in employee development is not confined to skill-building alone. It also plays a crucial role in mental and emotional growth. AI systems can provide employees with feedback that is neither delayed nor generic. Immediate feedback powered by AI helps employees to make on-the-spot adjustments and improvements, thereby accelerating their learning curve. This process of instant reflection and correction is a powerful driver of self-awareness and self-directed learning.

While AI-driven solutions are incredibly beneficial, they also pose certain challenges that need careful consideration. One of these challenges is ensuring the ethical use of AI in monitoring and evaluating employee performance. Privacy concerns and the risk of surveillance can lead to a work environment that lacks trust. To mitigate this, organizations must ensure transparency in how AI tools are used and involve employees in discussions about what data is collected and how it will be utilized. Ethical practices and data protection strategies must be at the forefront of AI implementation to maintain a balanced and respectful working environment.

Beyond ethical considerations, human judgment is indispensable in interpreting AI's recommendations. While AI can provide data-driven insights, the context and compassion that human input brings cannot be matched. Managers and leaders must be trained to complement AI's capabilities with their intuitive understanding of team dynamics and individual circumstances. In this way, AI becomes a powerful tool for informed decision-making, aiding leaders by providing diverse options rather than replacing the human touch.

As AI continues to redefine the scope of professional development, it draws upon an increasingly wide array of data sources. This data diversity enables a holistic view of employee growth, encompassing not just professional milestones but also personal development metrics such as communication skills and emotional intelligence. By focusing on comprehensive development, AI ensures that employees are well-rounded and equipped to handle diverse roles and responsibilities, thus enhancing their value to the organization.

It's equally important to recognize the psychological impact of AI-facilitated development. The empowerment that comes from having a clear, data-backed progression path can significantly boost employee morale and engagement. When employees see that their organization is invested in their growth, it fosters loyalty and can lead to higher retention rates. This is particularly pertinent as younger generations, such as Millennials and Gen Z, prioritize personal and professional growth in their career choices.

Furthermore, AI can bridge the geographical divides that often limit traditional development initiatives. Virtual reality training modules, language learning platforms, and cross-cultural competency courses powered by AI break down barriers, offering a global classroom experience. Such technologies enable remote teams to access the same quality and breadth of training as their on-site counterparts, ensuring consistency in development opportunities regardless of physical location.

While the benefits of using AI for employee development are manifold, organizations must remain vigilant of the limitations and biases that AI systems can inadvertently inherit. Continuous monitoring and updating of AI algorithms are crucial to ensure they remain fair and unbiased. An active approach to addressing bias, paired with diverse data input, can significantly minimize inaccuracies, thereby ensuring that AI-driven development is equitable for all employees.

Ultimately, the fusion of AI and employee development represents a reimagining of what growth means in the modern workplace. The key lies in balancing innovation with the age-old principles of empathy and understanding. Organizations that succeed in this endeavor are those that view AI as an enabler rather than a replacement, fostering an environment where technology enhances, rather than eclipses, the human spirit.

As we move forward, it's clear that AI's role in employee development will only expand. It will continue to reinvent the way we learn, adapt, and achieve. For leaders and employees alike, embracing this transformative power promises a future where personal growth and professional success are bound not by the constraints of technology, but enhanced by its potential to elevate. The journey is just beginning, and with AI's support, the opportunities for development are boundless.

Chapter 18:
The Role of AI in Corporate Social Responsibility

In the rapidly evolving landscape of AI-driven workplaces, leveraging artificial intelligence for corporate social responsibility (CSR) is becoming a game-changer. Organizations now have the opportunity to harness AI's capabilities to tackle pressing societal challenges, ranging from environmental sustainability to inclusive economic growth. AI tools can analyze complex data patterns and make accurate predictions, guiding businesses to make smarter, more ethical decisions. By aligning AI initiatives with CSR goals, companies can enhance transparency, drive social impact, and foster trust with stakeholders. This transformative approach not only improves brand reputation but also contributes to the long-term value creation that benefits both society and businesses. In an era where technology and social responsibility converge, AI stands as a powerful ally, offering innovative ways to address global issues while maintaining a competitive edge.

Leveraging AI for Social Good

Artificial Intelligence (AI), with its transformative prowess, extends beyond business efficiency and profit margins; it presents an unprecedented opportunity to advance social good. In today's fast-paced technological landscape, AI's potential to address complex societal challenges can't be overstated. From enhancing healthcare accessibility to fostering sustainable development, AI's role in promoting social welfare is rapidly expanding.

One of the most compelling uses of AI for social good is in healthcare. The ability to analyze and interpret vast amounts of data can revolutionize medical diagnostics and treatment plans. Algorithms that can detect diseases in early stages by analyzing medical images or predicting outbreaks of epidemics by processing health data globally signify a new era in preventive and personalized medicine. More than just improving medical outcomes, this AI-driven predictive power can reduce healthcare costs by prioritizing early intervention.

In education, AI is opening doors for more inclusive and accessible learning environments. Adaptive learning platforms harness AI algorithms to tailor educational content to each student's pace and style of learning, effectively personalizing curriculum materials. This level of customization ensures that students who might otherwise be left behind can thrive. Moreover, AI can bridge the educational gap in underserved areas by offering courses and materials in local languages and adapting content to regional needs.

AI's potential in improving environmental sustainability is equally promising. By analyzing data from satellite imagery, AI systems can monitor deforestation patterns, track wildlife populations, and predict climate changes. These insights allow for better-informed decisions regarding conservation strategies and policy-making. Moreover, AI-optimized resource management can lead to more efficient use of energy and water resources, contributing to a more sustainable and eco-friendly future. Imagine smart grids powered by AI algorithms reducing energy consumption or AI-driven logistics networks optimizing supply chains to cut emissions—each step a stride towards global sustainability.

The integration of AI into social services is transforming how assistance is administered. Chatbots equipped with natural language processing can provide immediate, accurate information to people in need, streamlining communication and access to essential services. Automating routine tasks in social welfare programs increases efficiency, allowing more resources and personnel to focus on complex cases requiring human attention.

One of the areas where AI's impact is particularly profound is in addressing economic disparities. AI can analyze financial data to offer insights into trends and patterns that were previously overlooked, paving the way for more targeted economic policies and interventions. By promoting transparency in financial markets and aiding in the creation of fair lending practices, AI is playing a crucial role in fostering economic equity.

Despite its benefits, leveraging AI for social good is not without challenges. Ethical considerations, such as maintaining data privacy and preventing algorithmic biases, remain paramount. The responsibility lies with researchers, policymakers, and corporations to ensure that AI applications respect human rights and are developed transparently. Implementing robust ethical frameworks and setting industry standards will help ensure that AI serves the public interest.

Collaboration stands at the heart of successful AI implementations for social good. Multidisciplinary teams involving data scientists, domain experts, and community stakeholders can foster innovation while ensuring that AI solutions are culturally sensitive and contextually relevant. International cooperation, sharing research, and building open-source platforms can significantly accelerate the development of AI tools aimed at addressing global issues.

Moreover, encouraging a culture of innovation in corporations can lead to the creation of AI-driven projects that prioritize social benefits. By aligning AI initiatives with corporate social responsibility (CSR) goals, businesses can not only enhance their brand reputation but also make tangible contributions to society. Companies like Microsoft and

Google have already committed resources towards AI projects that target pressing social issues, setting a precedent for industry-wide participation.

The economic implications of leveraging AI for social good are significant. By improving efficiencies, reducing waste, and addressing societal challenges, countries can bolster their economic resilience. Public-private partnerships can play a crucial role in this, encouraging investments in AI technologies that aim to benefit the broader community.

AI's role extends far beyond algorithmic prowess—it has the potential to usher in an era of change that prioritizes collective well-being over individual gains. We stand at the precipice of a technological frontier that, if navigated wisely, can lead to an era where technology directly contributes to the social fabric of communities worldwide. It's time to envision a future where AI is harnessed not only for its economic returns but as a pivotal tool for societal advancement.

Aligning AI Initiatives with CSR Goals

In today's rapidly transforming business landscape, the fusion of Artificial Intelligence (AI) with Corporate Social Responsibility (CSR) objectives isn't just a strategic advantage—it's an imperative. Organizations are under immense pressure from stakeholders, including consumers and investors, to not only harness the power of AI but also ensure that its applications reflect and enhance their commitment to CSR. Aligning AI initiatives with CSR goals poses unique challenges and opportunities, demanding a nuanced understanding of both domains to achieve meaningful outcomes.

AI technologies, when ethically designed and applied, can become powerful catalysts for promoting social good. As businesses commit to addressing pressing global challenges, from climate change to inequality, AI can offer intelligent solutions that traditional methods might fall short of providing. By integrating AI with CSR, organizations can analyze vast datasets to identify and predict societal needs with unprecedented accuracy, creating targeted strategies that contribute to their CSR objectives.

One of the primary ways AI can be aligned with CSR initiatives is through enhancing sustainability efforts. AI's capabilities in data analysis and pattern recognition can optimize resource usage, reduce waste, and enhance energy efficiency. For instance, AI-driven predictive analytics can analyze energy consumption patterns and suggest improvements, significantly reducing carbon footprints. Similarly, AI can help monitor and manage supply chains, ensuring that products are sourced ethically and that waste is minimized, thus supporting environmental sustainability goals.

Moreover, AI solutions can play a transformative role in addressing social inequality. Education and healthcare are two critical areas where AI's impact can be profound. By democratizing access to quality education through personalized learning platforms, AI can help bridge educational disparities. In healthcare, AI-driven tools can assist in diagnosing diseases early and optimizing treatment plans, especially in regions with limited access to medical professionals. These efforts, when integrated into a company's CSR strategy, demonstrate a genuine commitment to societal well-being and can lead to significant positive social impact.

However, the integration of AI with CSR goals is not without its complexities. Ethical considerations must be at the forefront to prevent exacerbating existing biases or creating new inequalities. For AI to truly align with CSR, its deployment must be guided by transparency and fairness principles. Organizations should ensure that AI algorithms are developed with diverse, representative data sets and continuously audited for bias. This oversight is crucial in building trust with stakeholders and ensuring that AI-driven initiatives genuinely reflect the company's CSR values.

The need for strategic leadership in navigating these challenges cannot be overstated. Business leaders must champion the alignment of AI and CSR from the top, instilling a corporate culture that prioritizes ethical AI practices. Cross-functional teams, blending expertise from technical, CSR, and ethical fields, should be established to govern AI initiatives, ensuring they align with broader CSR objectives. Such teams can provide invaluable insights into potential ethical pitfalls and societal impacts, establishing robust frameworks that guide AI development and deployment.

Embracing this alignment offers businesses a competitive advantage by enhancing their reputation and engaging stakeholders meaningfully. Consumers today are increasingly valuing ethical brands and are more likely to support companies that demonstrate genuine social responsibility through their actions. Thus, crafting AI initiatives that align with CSR can not only drive positive societal change but also resonate with a company's audience, deepening customer loyalty and trust.

It's also crucial that these initiatives are communicated effectively, both internally and externally. Transparency in the goals, processes, and outcomes of AI-driven CSR efforts is essential. Regular reporting on the impact of AI initiatives related to CSR can help maintain accountability and foster a culture of continuous improvement. Businesses can utilize various communication channels to share their stories, successes, and lessons learned, thereby encouraging wider industry adoption of similar practices.

Aligning AI initiatives with CSR goals paves the way for a future where technological advancement goes hand in hand with ethical responsibility. This balance is vital for the sustainable growth of businesses and the welfare of the society they operate within. As AI continues to evolve, its integration with CSR will be a defining factor in determining which organizations can navigate the complexities of modern business environments while upholding their commitment to creating a better world.

In summary, the convergence of AI and CSR holds transformative potential. By harnessing AI's capabilities to tackle social and environmental challenges thoughtfully and strategically, businesses can amplify their CSR efforts and create lasting, meaningful change. This alignment requires an unwavering commitment to ethics, robust leadership, and comprehensive strategies that ensure AI not only drives innovation but also supports a sustainable and equitable future.

Chapter 19:
AI-Enhanced Remote Work

As the nature of work transforms dramatically, AI emerges as both a catalyst and a conduit in redefining the conventionally understood boundaries of remote work. With AI-enhanced tools, teams find themselves collaborating more seamlessly than ever, shattering geographical barriers and fostering unprecedented connectivity. Sophisticated algorithms predict workflow bottlenecks and optimize schedules, allowing professionals to focus on creative problem-solving rather than mundane logistics. Yet, this brave new world isn't without its hurdles. Adapting to these technologies presents challenges in communication and team dynamics, offering opportunities for growth through resilience and learning. Leaders need to balance the scales, ensuring technology complements, rather than supersedes, human intuition and judgment. In doing so, they create a future where productivity and innovation coexist harmoniously with a sense of community, no matter the physical distance.

Tools and Technologies for Virtual Collaboration

In today's fast-paced world, the emergence of AI technologies has redefined how teams collaborate, especially in a virtual setting. Remote work, initially a necessity, has transformed into an integral part of modern business strategy. This shift demands adept tools and technologies to bridge geographical distances and disparate schedules.

At the heart of this transformation lies AI, enhancing and optimizing the remote work experience in ways previously unimaginable.

The adoption of AI in virtual collaboration tools has ushered in an era where productivity meets convenience. Platforms like Zoom, Microsoft Teams, and Slack have integrated AI functionalities to streamline operations. These tools aren't just about facilitating communication anymore; AI elevates them by providing real-time transcription, smart scheduling, and sentiment analysis. Such features enable better engagement and foster a collaborative environment even when team members are miles apart.

Consider, for instance, smart scheduling assistants powered by AI. These digital helpers evaluate multiple calendars, suggest optimal meeting times, and even consider time zones. Gone are the days of back-and-forth emails trying to set up a simple meeting. This level of efficiency not only saves time but also reduces friction among team members, allowing them to focus on creativity and innovation rather than logistics.

Another groundbreaking AI tool is transcription software that handles live meetings effortlessly. By converting discussions into text, these tools ensure everyone is on the same page, even if someone misses a meeting. Action items can be tracked more effectively, thanks to AI-driven analyses that highlight key points and tasks. This ensures a seamless transfer of information, reducing miscommunications that often arise in remote settings.

Virtual reality (VR) and augmented reality (AR) are also stepping into the realm of remote collaboration. These technologies redefine the meeting experience, allowing participants to interact in a shared virtual space. While still in their nascent stages, the potential for VR and AR to simulate in-person interactions can't be overstated. Imagine a design team sifting through 3D models or a marketing team brainstorming within a virtual boardroom – these experiences foster deeper collaboration and creativity.

AI-powered chatbots and virtual assistants have become indispensable in handling routine queries and tasks. Within collaborative platforms, they serve as a first line of support, providing instant information and guidance while learning from interactions to improve future responses. By automating repetitive tasks, AI allows teams to focus on strategic, high-impact work.

Document collaboration tools have also evolved with AI. Platforms like Google Workspace and Microsoft 365 leverage AI to offer intelligent document editing, data visualization, and predictive analytics. Features such as real-time editing, version control, and accessibility options ensure that all team members can contribute effectively. AI analyzes content to provide insights and recommendations, streamlining workflow and enhancing decision-making.

Moreover, AI's role in data security within collaborative tools can't be ignored. As data breaches rise, maintaining confidentiality in virtual spaces is paramount. AI enhances security protocols through anomaly detection and threat prediction, ensuring that sensitive information remains protected. This builds trust within remote teams, fostering a sense of security crucial for open communication.

AI also enables more personalized collaboration experiences. By analyzing past interactions, preferences, and work patterns, AI can suggest task prioritization, delegate duties, and tailor communication styles. This level of personalization boosts morale and allows team members to work in a manner best suited to their strengths, enhancing overall productivity.

Despite the promise and potential AI brings to virtual collaboration, organizations must remain cognizant of potential challenges. Ensuring equitable access to these tools is vital, as is addressing the learning curve associated with new technologies. Training programs and user-friendly interfaces can mitigate these barriers, facilitating smoother adoption and utilization.

As businesses continue to navigate the ever-evolving landscape of remote work, the integration of AI into collaboration tools will likely expand. Innovative technologies will continue to emerge, further dissolving the barriers of distance and time, and bringing people together in more meaningful ways. This evolution emphasizes that while the tools may change, the essence of collaboration — connection, communication, and co-creation — remains pivotal in driving success.

In the coming years, teams that can harness the full potential of AI-enhanced collaboration tools will find themselves at a decisive advantage. The organizations capable of nurturing a culture that embraces these technologies while remaining adaptable to future innovations will not only survive but thrive in the AI-driven age.

Challenges and Opportunities in Remote Work

The surge in remote work, fueled by rapid advancements in AI technologies, presents a tapestry of challenges and opportunities for businesses and professionals alike. While AI-enhanced tools have transformed remote work into a viable long-term trend, navigating its complexities requires a nuanced understanding of this ever-evolving landscape.

One of the most prominent challenges in AI-enhanced remote work is maintaining team cohesion and communication. In a traditional office environment, spontaneous interactions and organic collaboration often occur naturally. With remote work, however, teams can struggle with isolation and a lack of connection. AI-powered communication tools aim to bridge this gap by providing seamless virtual collaboration platforms. These tools incorporate natural language processing and machine learning to facilitate effective communication, manage projects, and keep team members aligned. Yet, the challenge remains in ensuring these tools don't inadvertently encourage a transactional rather than personable work culture.

Security and privacy concerns also loom large in the realm of remote work. As employees access sensitive company data from various locations, using multiple devices, the potential for security breaches increases. AI plays a critical role in enhancing cybersecurity measures, offering predictive analytics to foresee potential threats and automate responses. Nevertheless, companies must balance AI-driven security with employees' privacy rights, ensuring transparent data handling practices that foster trust rather than suspicion.

Opportunities in AI-enhanced remote work are manifold, particularly in the realm of democratizing access to talent. Organizations can now tap into a global talent pool, leveraging AI algorithms to match skill sets with job requirements efficiently. This expands the possibilities for both hiring managers and job seekers, creating a more dynamic and diverse workforce. However, this also necessitates a reevaluation of recruitment strategies to ensure equitable opportunities, taking into consideration the potential for algorithmic biases in AI-driven recruitment processes.

Notably, remote work environments amplified by AI afford unparalleled flexibility. Employees can tailor their work schedules to fit personal circumstances, potentially leading to increased satisfaction and productivity. However, the expectation for perpetual availability can blur the lines between work and personal life, creating challenges around maintaining work-life balance. Companies must establish clear boundaries and expectations, using AI to monitor workloads and prevent burnout while empowering employees to take control of their work patterns.

AI's capability in automating routine tasks presents another dual-edged sword in remote work. On one hand, by freeing employees from mundane tasks, AI allows them to focus on higher-value activities, fostering creativity and innovation. On the other hand, this raises concerns about job displacement and the need for continuous skill development to remain relevant in an AI-dominated job market. Thus, there is a crucial opportunity for businesses to invest in upskilling and reskilling programs, encouraging a culture of lifelong learning.

Another significant opportunity lies in redefining performance evaluation and feedback processes. AI tools can analyze employee performance metrics with an unprecedented level of accuracy and objectivity. This enables a more data-driven approach to performance reviews, helping to eliminate bias and subjectivity. However, the challenge is to ensure that performance metrics reflect true value contribution and do not encourage counterproductive behaviors. Emphasizing qualitative feedback alongside quantitative data is vital to maintain a holistic view of employee performance.

Moreover, AI stands to revolutionize remote workspaces themselves. Intelligent systems can suggest optimal workflows and environmental adjustments to enhance productivity. Virtual reality (VR) and augmented reality (AR) powered by AI could simulate almost real office-like experiences, offering immersive collaboration opportunities irrespective of physical location. Yet, the challenge remains in making these technologies accessible and intuitive for all employees, mitigating any digital divides that may arise from varying tech literacy levels.

In conclusion, while AI-enhanced remote work presents a host of challenges, it equally offers numerous opportunities to innovate and reimagine the work environment. Companies that successfully navigate these dynamics will not only maintain competitiveness but will thrive by fostering an inclusive, dynamic, and resilient workforce.

Future leaders must be agile, continually adapting to the changes AI brings, while prioritizing human connections and ethical considerations in their strategic decisions. The journey may be complex, but with thoughtful implementation, the integration of AI in remote work can usher in a new era of organizational success and employee empowerment.

Chapter 20:
Data Privacy and Security
in the AI Era

In a world that increasingly leans on AI for innovation and efficiency, safeguarding data privacy and ensuring robust security protocols have become paramount. As AI systems expand, they harness vast quantities of data, presenting both remarkable opportunities and significant challenges. Professionals today must prioritize the protection of sensitive information while balancing the drive for technological advancement. With new AI threats emerging, vigilance and strategic countermeasures are critical. Organizations need to cultivate an environment where data security is integrated into the core of their AI operations. This fusion not only protects assets but also fosters trust and maintains compliance with evolving regulations. Navigating this landscape requires a proactive approach, blending understanding with foresight to ensure data not only fuels AI innovation but does so securely. By doing so, businesses can thrive, leveraging AI responsibly while upholding the values of privacy and security in this transformative era.

Protecting Sensitive Information

As we stand on the precipice of the AI era, the importance of protecting sensitive information cannot be overstated. In today's data-driven world, where information is both an asset and a liability, businesses and individuals alike are challenged to strike a balance between leveraging data for innovation and safeguarding it against misuse. The rapid pace of AI development has opened up a plethora of opportunities but also poses significant risks that must be thoughtfully managed.

Protecting sensitive information is not just about technical measures; it's also about cultivating a culture of awareness and accountability. Businesses need to prioritize data privacy and security as a critical component of their overall strategy. This involves not only implementing robust security protocols but also fostering an environment where every stakeholder is educated about the importance of data protection. The goal is to embed security into the DNA of the organization, so it becomes a natural consideration in every decision-making process.

One of the first steps in protecting sensitive data is identifying what constitutes as sensitive within the unique context of each organization. While general categories such as personal information, financial data, and proprietary information are universally recognized, nuances exist depending on industry and jurisdiction. Organizations must conduct comprehensive data audits to map the flow of information and identify where vulnerabilities might lie. This forms the foundation for developing robust data protection strategies tailored to specific operational realities.

The implementation of encryption technology is a critical defense mechanism in the protection of sensitive information. Encryption ensures that data remains indecipherable to unauthorized users, providing a layer of security even if a data breach occurs. By encrypting sensitive data both in transit and at rest, organizations can significantly reduce the risk of unauthorized access. However, it's essential to continuously update encryption methods to counter evolving threats, ensuring that they remain effective against sophisticated attacks.

In addition to encryption, deploying access control measures is vital. Not everyone within an organization needs access to every piece of information. By implementing role-based access control, organizations can ensure that employees only have access to the data necessary for their roles. This principle of least privilege minimizes the risk of data leakage and ensures accountability, as actions with sensitive data can be traced back to specific individuals.

Moreover, the advent of artificial intelligence itself can be leveraged to bolster data protection efforts. AI-driven tools can now proactively detect anomalies in data access patterns, flagging potential breaches before they occur. These systems can analyze vast amounts of data in real-time, identifying threats with greater speed and accuracy than human capability alone. By integrating AI into their security infrastructures, businesses can achieve a dynamic defense posture that adapts to emerging threats.

However, reliance on AI for security is not without its challenges. AI systems must be meticulously trained to understand complex data threats and avoid false positives that can lead to unnecessary disruption. The ethical use of AI in security also requires that these systems respect individuals' privacy and operate transparently. It is crucial that organizations provide clear guidelines and maintain human oversight to ensure AI's use in security aligns with broader ethical standards.

Additionally, compliance with legal and regulatory frameworks is a key aspect of protecting sensitive information. The increasing number of data privacy laws, such as the General Data Protection Regulation (GDPR) in Europe and the California Consumer Privacy Act (CCPA) in the United States, mandates stringent data protection measures. Non-compliance can lead to severe penalties and damage to a company's reputation. Organizations must stay informed about regulatory changes and invest in compliance programs to manage these evolving obligations effectively.

Educating and training employees about data privacy is another crucial component in protecting sensitive information. Security protocols and technology are only as effective as the people who use them. Regular training sessions can ensure that employees are aware of the latest data protection policies and understand their role in safeguarding data. Empowering employees with knowledge about cybersecurity threats, such as phishing and social engineering, can mitigate risks by preventing security breaches at the user level.

Another important aspect is developing incident response plans that outline procedures to follow in the event of a data breach. These plans should be comprehensive yet flexible, detailing specific roles and responsibilities while allowing for adaptation to the unique circumstances of each incident. By conducting regular drills and simulations, organizations can ensure they are prepared to respond swiftly and effectively, minimizing the impact of data breaches on operations and reputation.

Lastly, fostering partnerships and collaborations with other organizations can enhance an entity's ability to protect sensitive information. By participating in industry consortiums and sharing best practices, businesses can stay ahead of emerging threats and develop stronger defense mechanisms. Collaboration with other organizations can lead to innovative solutions that improve data protection not only within the organization but across the industry.

The responsibility of protecting sensitive information in the AI era is profound but achievable. As AI continues to transform every facet of work, its role in data privacy and security will become only more pronounced. By approaching this challenge with a strategic, yet flexible mindset, organizations can not only protect their sensitive information but gain a competitive advantage in today's interconnected world. In doing so, they will build a future where innovation thrives in an environment of trust and security.

AI Threats and Countermeasures

As we delve into the intersection of artificial intelligence and data security, the urgency of addressing AI-related threats becomes increasingly apparent. The sheer magnitude of data processed by AI systems each day is staggering, and as these systems grow ever more capable, they simultaneously enlarge the attack surface for potential data breaches, fraud, and other cybersecurity risks.

One of the primary concerns is the misuse of AI technologies. With AI's power to analyze vast datasets quickly, there's a risk it could be harnessed for nefarious purposes, such as automating cyber-attacks or creating advanced phishing schemes. These AI-driven attacks can adapt in real-time, presenting a sinister challenge for traditional security measures. AI algorithms could also be exploited to identify and exploit system vulnerabilities faster than human hackers ever could.

Beside external threats, there's the potential for AI systems to internally compromise data privacy through unintended biases in machine learning models. These biases might result from skewed training data, leading to unfair or inaccurate outcomes. Such issues can tarnish a company's reputation and lead to significant legal ramifications. The complexity and opacity of AI models often exacerbate this problem, making it difficult to interpret AI-driven decisions and to hold systems accountable.

To counteract these threats, organizations must adopt a multi-layered approach to security. This begins with designing AI systems with a strong emphasis on transparency and fairness. Ensuring ethical AI requires not just tech experts, but interdisciplinary collaboration among ethicists, legal professionals, and domain experts. Furthermore, employing techniques like explainable AI can demystify how decisions are made. When stakeholders understand the decision-making process, trust is enhanced, and biases can be more easily spotted and rectified.

Another robust countermeasure involves the implementation of AI for defensive purposes. Just as AI can be used in offensive cyber tactics, it holds potential for strengthening cybersecurity defenses. AI-driven tools can detect anomalies and flag suspicious activities more effectively than traditional systems. By continuously monitoring network traffic and user behaviors, AI can provide an early warning system against potential threats.

Nonetheless, deploying AI for security isn't without its challenges. These systems require constant updating and maintenance to cope with ever-evolving threats. The training data for these AI security systems must be meticulously curated to avoid introducing bias or blind spots that could be exploited. Moreover, while AI systems can process data at previously unimaginable speeds, the decisions they make should always be subject to human oversight to ensure they align with organizational goals and ethical standards.

Regular audits and risk assessments of AI systems are crucial. These help organizations identify weaknesses and areas for improvement, ensuring that security measures evolve alongside threats. It is also imperative to conduct thorough penetration testing to simulate attacks and ascertain the resilience of AI systems under duress. Companies should establish protocols for incident response, highlighting procedures for identifying, containing, and mitigating breaches or other security incidents.

In addition to technical measures, fostering a culture of cybersecurity awareness is vital. Employees should be trained to recognize potential threats and understand the importance of data protection. Routine security training sessions can ensure that staff remains vigilant and informed about the latest phishing tactics and social engineering ploys.

International collaboration is another pillar in fortifying AI security. As AI transcends geographical boundaries, international regulatory bodies should work in unison to tackle AI threats on a global scale. Such cooperation can lead to the development of comprehensive frameworks for AI governance, informed by diverse perspectives and aligning with global ethical standards.

Lastly, organizations must invest in cutting-edge research to stay ahead of would-be attackers. By staying informed about the latest advancements in AI and cybersecurity, businesses can anticipate emerging threats and rapidly adapt their security strategies. Such forward-thinking approaches are key to protecting sensitive information in an era where AI's capabilities are continuously expanding.

The journey toward robust AI security is complex, yet critical. As AI continues to integrate deeper into the fabric of our digital world, ensuring its safe use demands vigilance, innovation, and broad-spectrum collaboration. With these multidimensional strategies, the goal of safeguarding data privacy and security in the AI era becomes not just feasible, but achievable.

Chapter 21:
AI in Supply Chain and Logistics

The transformative potential of AI in supply chain and logistics is nothing short of revolutionary. Imagine a network of intelligent algorithms that seamlessly predict demand, optimize routes, and manage inventory levels in real-time, all while increasing efficiency and reducing costs. Companies today leverage AI to enhance operational decisions, drawing on vast amounts of data to identify patterns and areas for improvement. This shift isn't merely about automation—it's about creating a responsive, resilient supply chain capable of adapting to market shifts and disruptions. By integrating AI, businesses unlock the ability to predict potential bottlenecks and optimize supply flows, ensuring that the right products reach consumers with precision like never before. In a world where speed and accuracy can make or break a business, AI-driven supply chains represent not only a technological advancement but a strategic imperative for future success.

Optimizing Supply Chain Operations

In today's fast-paced and globalized market, supply chain operations are the backbone of successful businesses. Organizations are constantly looking for ways to enhance these operations for efficiency, resilience, and sustainability. Enter Artificial Intelligence (AI), a transformative force reshaping supply chains with its ability to analyze vast amounts of data and provide insights that drive innovation. AI optimizes supply chain tasks from demand forecasting to logistics, offering unprecedented visibility and precision.

Supply chain management involves intricate networks of suppliers, manufacturers, distributors, and retailers working in alignment to move products from their origin to the end consumer. This complexity often introduces challenges like predicting demand fluctuations, managing inventories, and ensuring timely deliveries. Here, AI steps in to revolutionize traditional methods. By utilizing machine learning algorithms, AI can predict demand patterns more accurately than ever before, allowing companies to prepare for market changes ahead of time.

One of the immediate benefits of AI in supply chain operations is the improvement in demand forecasting. Traditional forecasting methods, which often rely on historical data, can be shortsighted, especially in volatile markets. AI integrates real-time data, including social media trends, economic indicators, and even weather patterns, to create a more comprehensive forecast. This predictive power helps businesses reduce waste, optimize stock levels, and ensure they have the right products in the right quantities at the right time.

Optimizing inventory management is yet another domain where AI shines. Automated systems can track inventory levels, orders, and deliveries, reducing human error and freeing up resources for more strategic tasks. With AI-powered inventory management, businesses can maintain lean inventories while minimizing the risk of stockouts and overstock situations. The ripple effect of such precise control extends to cost savings, enhanced customer satisfaction, and improved cash flow management.

AI's impact doesn't stop at the warehouse or distribution center. In logistics, AI optimizes routes and manages deliveries, ensuring goods reach their destination efficiently. By analyzing factors like traffic patterns, transportation costs, and environmental conditions,

AI systems suggest optimal routes, reducing delivery times and costs. This level of intelligence not only boosts efficiency but also contributes to sustainability efforts by cutting downtime and lowering carbon emissions.

The journey from a plant to the store shelf is fraught with uncertainties. However, AI introduces a layer of predictability and control. For instance, if a natural disaster disrupts a supply chain node, AI algorithms can quickly reroute shipments, minimizing delays. These reactive capabilities are essential in today's uncertain geopolitical climate, where supply chain resilience can be the difference between thriving and failing businesses.

Moreover, AI-driven operational efficiencies sometimes lead to competitive advantages that weren't previously possible. As businesses lean into AI, they find new ways to differentiate themselves in crowded markets. They can offer faster delivery times or guaranteed product availability and thus forge deeper bonds with their customers. It's a transformation that doesn't just meet customers' expectations but often exceeds them.

However, the AI revolution in supply chain optimization isn't without its hurdles. Implementing these technologies requires substantial investment, both financially and in terms of time and resource allocation. Organizations must consider the integration of AI systems with existing processes and infrastructure. The transition might demand new skill sets and cultural shifts within companies. Success hinges not just on the technology itself but on leadership that understands the potential of AI and nurtures an environment open to change.

Data security emerges as a paramount concern as more operations become increasingly automated. With AI systems relying on vast datasets, ensuring the privacy of sensitive information becomes critical. Companies must adopt robust cybersecurity measures and remain vigilant to protect data integrity and prevent breaches. Transparency in AI methodologies can also bolster trust among partners and customers.

Furthermore, an AI-driven supply chain raises moral and ethical questions. Automation and algorithm-driven decisions might lead to job displacement in some roles, posing workforce challenges. Thus, organizations must strike a balance, employing AI to augment human capabilities rather than replace them. Training programs focused on upskilling employees ensure that people remain integral to the supply chain's future.

As businesses continue to integrate AI into their supply chain operations, we stand on the cusp of a new era marked by unprecedented efficiency and innovation. The potential for growth is immense, yet it must be managed thoughtfully and responsibly. Those who can harness the power of AI while navigating its challenges are poised to lead the next chapter of supply chain evolution. With each advancement, AI convinces us of what is possible when technology and logistics work hand in hand, crafting a future where supply chain operations are not only optimized but also resilient and sustainable.

AI-Driven Inventory Management

In the complex world of supply chains, inventory management is a critical factor that can make or break a business's efficiency and profitability. Traditionally, inventory management has relied heavily on manual oversight and basic algorithms. However, the emergence of artificial intelligence (AI) is rapidly transforming how companies approach this crucial function.

AI-driven inventory management systems are designed to tackle the perennial challenges of overstocking, stockouts, and unsold inventory. By incorporating machine learning algorithms, these systems can analyze massive datasets—from historic sales figures to real-time market trends—resulting in more accurate demand forecasting. This data-driven approach enables businesses to optimize their inventory levels, reduce holding costs, and ensure that products are available when customers need them.

At the heart of AI-driven inventory management is predictive analytics. Unlike traditional statistical models, AI algorithms can consider an array of complex factors—seasonal trends, economic indicators, marketing campaigns, and more—to predict future demand. This holistic analysis provides a level of precision that is simply unattainable through manual methods.

Moreover, AI is particularly adept at identifying patterns and anomalies in data that human analysts might overlook. For instance, suppose an unexpected change in consumer behavior begins to unfold due to a viral trend on social media. In that case, AI systems can swiftly detect these shifts and adjust inventory levels accordingly. This real-time adaptability is crucial in an era where consumer preferences can pivot with remarkable speed.

An additional benefit of AI is its capacity to automate routine tasks involved in inventory management, such as counting stock or reordering products. This automation frees up human resources, allowing employees to focus on more strategic, higher-value activities. Integrating AI doesn't just enhance efficiency; it also transforms the role of supply chain professionals, requiring them to work alongside these intelligent systems and leverage their insights.

Inventory optimization through AI involves not just maintaining the right stock levels but also ensuring that the inventory is suitably distributed across different locations. AI uses dynamic data inputs to recommend distribution strategies, ensuring products are strategically positioned to meet demand swiftly and efficiently. This is particularly important in today's world of global logistics, where delays can significantly impact customer satisfaction and overall business performance.

AI-driven inventory management systems also enhance accuracy in various aspects of the inventory lifecycle. Advanced image recognition technology can automate the inspection process, ensuring quality control by identifying defective or incorrect products before they reach customers. Such advancements reduce error rates and enhance customer experience, aligning well with overarching business goals.

Another noteworthy advantage is the implementation of autonomous inventory management systems in warehousing. Robotics equipped with AI capabilities can navigate storage facilities, perform stock checks, and facilitate retrieval processes without human intervention. These systems work non-stop, significantly speeding up operations and decreasing the likelihood of manual errors.

The environmental implications of AI-driven inventory management cannot be overlooked, either. By optimizing inventory levels and distribution, businesses can reduce waste and minimize their carbon footprint. The AI systems facilitate efficient resource utilization by ensuring that materials and products are used judiciously, aligning operational goals with sustainability initiatives.

Yet, like all technologies, AI-driven inventory management systems are not without their challenges. Data integrity remains a critical focus. The effectiveness of AI systems hinges on the quality and reliability of the data being utilized. Inconsistent or inaccurate data can lead to flawed analyses and decisions. Thus, establishing robust data management practices is essential for businesses to reap the full benefits of AI.

Additionally, the adoption of AI in inventory management necessitates a cultural shift within organizations. Employees must be retrained to embrace AI-driven insights and modify conventional practices in light of new data and intelligence. This requires strong leadership and a willingness to evolve, encouraging a mindset that perceives AI as a tool for enhancement rather than replacement.

Security considerations are also paramount when incorporating AI into inventory management. As with any digital system, there is a risk of cyber threats, necessitating comprehensive security measures to protect sensitive business data and maintain operational integrity.

Ultimately, the value of AI-driven inventory management systems lies in their ability to transform constraints into opportunities. Businesses can turn the challenges of fluctuating demand, supply chain disruptions, and customer expectations into competitive advantages. By harnessing the power of AI, companies not only improve their inventory processes but also pave the way for more resilient, efficient, and adaptable supply chains.

The future of inventory management is indeed bright. As AI technologies continue to evolve and mature, their integration into supply chain logistics will become increasingly seamless and sophisticated. Businesses that embrace and invest in AI-driven inventory management today are well-positioned to lead in their industries tomorrow, leveraging newfound intelligence to drive innovation and success in the ever-evolving marketplace.

Chapter 22:
Harnessing AI for Innovation

In the rapidly evolving landscape of modern business, the key to staying ahead lies in the ability to harness the transformative power of artificial intelligence for fostering innovation. AI offers unparalleled tools for accelerating research and development, enabling companies to prototype and iterate more swiftly than ever before. By leveraging advanced algorithms and machine learning, businesses can unlock creative potential, breaking down traditional barriers to ideation and execution. From generating new product ideas to optimizing existing processes, AI empowers organizations to envisage possibilities that were once thought impractical. Through this synergy of human ingenuity and artificial intelligence, businesses not only streamline operations but also inspire a culture of perpetual innovation. Embracing AI as a cornerstone of the innovation process allows us to anticipate change and boldly create the future, rather than merely adapting to it.

Accelerating Research and Development

In the bustling age of AI, research and development (R&D) no longer follow the conventional routes. Today's landscape sees AI as a catalyst, propelling innovation at unprecedented speeds. While once researchers relied heavily on human intuition and laborious experimentation, AI now acts as both a partner and a tool, navigating complex data landscapes and generating insights with unparalleled precision.

Startups and established companies alike are harnessing AI to fast-track the development of new products, medicines, and technologies. By automating data collection and analysis, AI reduces the time from concept to prototype, enabling businesses to innovate and iterate rapidly. Take pharmaceuticals, for example. Traditional drug discovery often spanned over a decade, but now, AI algorithms can sift through vast biological data sets, identify patterns, and suggest compounds in a fraction of the time. This capability is invaluable in areas demanding swift responses, like outbreaks of new diseases.

Beyond speed, AI introduces an exploratory depth that can be transformative. With machine learning models capable of predicting outcomes of numerous hypothetical scenarios, researchers can simulate trial and error without the significant costs of physical experimentation. This kind of virtual R&D environment means that potential projects can be vetted far more thoroughly before any resources are committed to real-world testing. Moreover, AI doesn't just make the old processes faster; it fundamentally shifts the paradigm of what is possible in R&D.

Innovation today has a diverse toolkit, of which AI has become an indispensable component. In sectors such as material science, AI assists in discovering novel materials by predicting molecular properties with high accuracy before materials are synthesized. Researchers can thus focus efforts on the most promising candidates, conserving both time and resources. It's a game of precision and possibility, one where AI lays the groundwork for breakthroughs that might have seemed improbable just a decade ago.

AI-driven R&D fosters a culture of innovation that is iterative and inclusive. It democratizes access to sophisticated analytical tools, allowing smaller institutions with limited resources to participate in groundbreaking research. This inclusivity broadens the range of potential innovations, pushing boundaries further and faster than rigid hierarchies and traditional silos ever could. The playing field is leveled, as data and AI-powered insights become accessible to those beyond the typical power centers of innovation.

While the efficiency gains brought by AI are indisputable, they also present unique challenges. The rapid pace of innovation necessitates a recalibration of ethical and safety standards. How do we ensure that we maintain rigorous testing protocols when AI significantly shortens testing cycles? There's a balance to be struck between innovation and caution, necessitating new frameworks and guidelines for responsible AI adoption in R&D.

Moreover, the reliance on AI systems introduces challenges around data integrity and algorithmic transparency. Decisions based on AI can only be as good as the data feeding into these systems. Organizations must prioritize data accuracy and integrity, ensuring that their AI models are not only powerful but also fair and unbiased. Transparency in AI processes is crucial for maintaining trust, especially since many R&D activities have profound implications on public welfare.

Harnessing AI for R&D is as much about embracing new strategies as it is about rethinking existing models of collaboration. AI itself is a landscape requiring constant cultivation and monitoring. We must foster interdisciplinary cooperation, bringing together data scientists, subject experts, and ethicists to navigate the complexities AI presents. This conjugation of expertise ensures that innovations are not only technically robust but also grounded in ethical principles.

At its heart, the accelerated pace of R&D in the age of AI is a testament to human ambition and ingenuity. AI presents tools of immense power, and with these tools, there's a responsibility to direct innovation towards outcomes that benefit society at large. As we stand at the forefront of this technological revolution, the task is to steer this vehicle of change along paths that align with our shared values and aspirations.

The possibility space AI opens for R&D is virtually limitless. As businesses and researchers continue to push theoretical boundaries, we approach an era where the pace of development is only matched by our imagination. AI facilitates a form of creative problem-solving unhampered by traditional constraints, enabling us to conceptualize and construct a future faster than we ever thought possible.

In summary, AI doesn't just accelerate R&D—it transforms it. By allowing us to iterate quickly, explore broadly, and collaborate effectively, AI is not just a tool of innovation, but a forge. It shapes the processes that will define the next generation of progress, ensuring that humanity doesn't remain tethered to the present, but reaches confidently toward the horizon of potential that AI points us toward.

Unlocking Creative Potential with AI

In an era where artificial intelligence continues to redefine the boundaries of technology and creativity, unlocking the creative potential with AI has emerged as a transformative force for businesses and individuals alike. The fusion of AI and creativity isn't just a future possibility; it's an ongoing revolution that's reshaping how we innovate, design, and imagine new possibilities. By transcending traditional creative boundaries, AI has opened up new dimensions for artistic expression, design thinking, and problem-solving.

AI's ability to analyze vast amounts of data at unprecedented speeds gives it a distinct edge in creative processes. While human creativity thrives in nuanced and abstract thinking, AI complements this by providing data-driven insights that can inspire new directions and ideas. This synergy between AI and human creativity has led to innovations in various fields—from art and design to marketing and product development. By processing massive datasets, AI algorithms can detect patterns, predict trends, and suggest innovative approaches that humans may overlook due to cognitive biases or limitations.

The creative industry, which includes sectors like entertainment, advertising, and digital media, is particularly witnessing the power of AI. Creative professionals are leveraging AI tools to develop immersive experiences and personalized content. For instance, AI-driven video editing software can automatically generate trailers based on audience preferences, making content creation more efficient while also enhancing the consumer experience. By analyzing audience data, content creators can tailor their works to specific target groups, improving engagement and satisfaction.

Furthermore, AI is propelling experimentation in the arts. Artists are using AI tools to generate music, visual art, and even literature. Programs like DeepArt, OpenAI's GPT models, and Amper Music allow creators to blend code with creativity, producing unique and groundbreaking art pieces. This intersection of technology and art not only democratizes creativity by making sophisticated tools more accessible but also challenges traditional perceptions of originality and authorship.

In design and architecture, AI has become an invaluable tool for ideation and prototyping. AI systems can analyze spatial data and customer preferences to propose structures that are not only aesthetically pleasing but also functionally optimized. This capability allows architects and designers to visualize and iterate on designs in ways that were previously inconceivable. Moreover, AI-driven generative design tools take input on constraints and deliver numerous design alternatives, thereby expanding the realm of what's possible.

As businesses seek to innovate, integrating AI into their creative processes can lead to substantial competitive advantages. AI can automate routine tasks, enabling creative teams to focus on higher-level work and innovation. For instance, AI's ability to quickly process feedback and revise content can drastically reduce time-to-market for new campaigns and products. By incorporating AI into their toolkits, marketing teams can develop data-driven strategies with compelling storytelling that's backed by insights rather than assumptions.

The implications of AI-enhanced creativity extend beyond products and services to transformation in organizational culture. Companies aspiring to boost innovation must foster an environment that embraces AI as a collaborator rather than a competitor. This shift involves redefining roles where AI tools enhance human creativity, providing employees with the freedom to explore bolder ideas, take creative risks, and push the boundaries of what's possible. This collaborative dynamic not only drives innovation but can also attract talent eager to work at the cutting edge of technology and creativity.

However, while the potential of AI in creativity is vast, it also raises important ethical and philosophical considerations. As AI systems play a more prominent role in creative processes, questions regarding bias, ownership, and authenticity come to the forefront. Ensuring that AI-driven creativity remains ethical and inclusive is paramount. For businesses, this means establishing guidelines to mitigate biases in AI-generated content and actively fostering diversity in datasets and algorithms.

Moreover, legal frameworks and intellectual property laws must evolve to address this new landscape. The role AI plays in the creation of content challenges existing notions of copyright and ownership, necessitating new paradigms that reflect the collaborative nature of human-AI endeavors. Businesses and creators must engage in open discussions about these issues to develop fair and equitable solutions.

AI is not a replacement for human creativity, but a tool that extends its possibilities. By embracing this technology, individuals and organizations can explore uncharted territories, catalyze innovation, and create outcomes that are more impactful than ever before. The key to unlocking AI's creative potential lies in continuous learning and adaptation, fostering a mindset that thrives on exploration and embraces the fusion of technology and imagination.

In conclusion, as AI continues to integrate with creative fields, it promises to reshape how we think about creativity itself. The journey towards unlocking the full creative potential of AI is dynamic and ongoing, requiring a balance between innovation and ethics. By utilizing AI as a creative partner, society stands to benefit from previously unimaginable opportunities in fostering innovation that'll redefine our future.

Chapter 23:
Measuring AI's Impact on
Business Performance

In the rapidly evolving landscape of AI-driven businesses, quantifying the effectiveness of AI initiatives is critical to ensuring they're not just innovations for the sake of it but true drivers of business success. Companies can no longer rely solely on traditional metrics; instead, they must embrace new analytics designed to measure the nuanced impacts of AI on performance. This includes understanding how AI influences decision-making efficiency, customer engagement, and overall productivity. By integrating advanced data analytics with AI, businesses can establish benchmarks that provide a clear view of AI's contribution to their strategic goals. These benchmarks not only measure success but also guide continuous improvement, ensuring AI implementations are dynamically aligned with the business's evolving objectives. Motivated by these insights, leaders are equipped to make informed choices that drive growth and foster a competitive edge in the market, making AI's integration a strategic triumph rather than a technological curiosity.

Metrics and Analytics for AI Assessment

The transformative potential of artificial intelligence in the workplace is undeniable. To harness this potential effectively, organizations must employ precise metrics and analytics to assess AI's impact on business performance. This is not just about proving value; it's about continuous improvement and gaining insights that drive strategic decisions. To truly understand AI's influence, businesses need to employ a multi-faceted approach, balancing quantitative indicators with qualitative insights. As we delve into the various methods for evaluating AI's contributions, consider the nuances of how these metrics can paint a comprehensive picture of your AI initiatives.

Setting clear objectives for what you aim to achieve with AI is the first step. Once these goals are established, it becomes essential to identify key performance indicators (KPIs) that align with these objectives. These metrics should be tailored to the organization's specific context and deliver insights into how AI technologies influence both operational efficiency and strategic outcomes. Common KPIs include cost reduction, time savings, error rates, and increases in revenue or productivity. However, organizations often need to dig deeper to unearth the less obvious impacts such as customer satisfaction, employee engagement, or innovation rates.

Operational metrics look at AI's ability to streamline processes and improve efficiency. Reduction in process cycle times, enhanced accuracy through predictive analytics, and automation of routine tasks are some direct metrics that can indicate AI effectiveness. While operational metrics give a concrete measure of improvement in processes, they are part of a larger ecosystem that interacts with the organization's strategic goals and cultural shifts.

Quantitative analysis provides a measurable view, but numbers alone can fall short of telling the whole story. Qualitative insights add depth to these figures, offering a narrative around employee experiences and customer interactions. Conducting surveys and interviews with employees and customers can provide valuable feedback on how AI solutions are perceived and the satisfaction they deliver. These insights often reveal aspects such as user-friendliness, empowerment, and morale that numbers alone cannot capture.

Dashboards and visualization tools play a crucial role in making these metrics actionable. They turn raw data into insightful visual representations, enabling stakeholders to see trends, outliers, and patterns at a glance. Effective dashboards are customizable and interactive, providing users the ability to drill down into specific areas of interest for more detailed analysis. Well-designed dashboards not only help track progress but also foster data-driven cultures within organizations by making information accessible and understandable.

Aside from internal metrics, benchmarking against industry standards is another vital component of assessing AI's business impact. By comparing performance metrics with industry peers, organizations can identify where they stand in terms of AI maturity and capability. This external perspective can highlight both strengths and areas for improvement, catalyzing strategic initiatives that elevate competitiveness. Strategic alliances and industry consortiums can offer platforms for sharing best practices and learning from the successes and challenges of others.

The dynamic nature of AI requires ongoing assessment rather than one-off evaluations. Continuous monitoring frameworks, which incorporate regular feedback loops, help organizations remain agile and responsive to changes. Adopting a cycle of iterative assessment can uncover new opportunities to refine AI applications and respond to evolving market demands swiftly. This iterative approach is akin to agile methodologies used in software development, where incremental improvements are constantly applied.

Advanced analytics, such as machine learning and artificial neural networks, can enhance the assessment process by identifying patterns and correlations that might not be immediately visible. These analytics techniques can provide predictive insights into future performance trends and simulate scenarios that help in strategic planning. By leveraging cutting-edge analytics, businesses can not only assess current impacts but also forecast future potential, driving long-term success.

Finally, the ethical aspect of AI cannot be ignored. Metrics should also factor in ethical considerations and the social responsibility aspects of AI usage. Transparency and accountability in AI decision-making processes, as well as the impact on job roles and societal welfare, often require additional metrics that these functions assess. Ensuring AI applications align with the organization's values and contribute positively to society mitigates risks and fosters trust among stakeholders.

In conclusion, the effective assessment of AI's impact on business performance requires a robust metrics and analytics framework. This includes both quantitative and qualitative measures, enhanced by ongoing analysis, visualization, and ethical considerations. As organizations continue to evolve in their AI maturity, these assessments provide a pathway to maximize AI's potential, ultimately yielding strategic value and competitive advantages in the dynamic business landscape.

Benchmarking AI-Enabled Success

As businesses continue to integrate AI into their operations, understanding what defines success becomes not just helpful but essential. Simply adopting AI technologies doesn't guarantee improved performance or profitability. Just as in any strategic initiative, the key lies in effectively benchmarking the impacts and results of AI systems. This involves not only identifying the right metrics but also analyzing those metrics with an understanding of the nuanced ways AI can transform business dynamics.

Benchmarking AI-enabled success begins with the identification and implementation of precise and relevant metrics. Traditional business performance indicators, such as revenue growth, cost reduction, and market share, still hold significant value. Yet, AI introduces a new suite of metrics that leaders must consider. Metrics such as accuracy, precision, recall, and algorithmic performance are increasingly relevant to evaluate AI capabilities. But it doesn't stop there. Contextual effectiveness—how well AI aligns with and supports specific business objectives—is also crucial. Companies must tailor their benchmarking to reflect not only industry standards but also their unique goals and processes.

Once metrics are defined, the real work begins: continuous measurement and analysis. Tracking the operational efficiency of AI systems, for instance, can reveal how much time and resources are being saved. These insights allow businesses to calibrate their AI solutions, ensuring they streamline operations without compromising quality or creativity. Moreover, examining data on customer interactions with AI platforms helps to gauge user satisfaction and adoption, which are critical for long-term success. By fostering a culture of measurement and feedback, organizations can translate raw data into actionable insights.

Transparency and accountability are indispensable in the benchmarking process. Enterprises must ensure that their AI systems operate ethically and transparently, minimizing biases and errors. Clear frameworks for monitoring and reporting AI systems' performance should be in place. Ensuring accountability not only helps in compliance with legal standards but also strengthens trust with stakeholders, from employees to customers. In a world increasingly wary of automation's ethical implications, transparency and accountability serve as ethical safeguards in AI deployment.

Central to every successful AI initiative is the alignment with strategic goals. Benchmarks ought to be closely linked to an organization's broader objectives, supporting its vision and long-term strategy. Success in AI is best achieved when technology supports mission-critical activities and creates value in line with core business aspirations. This alignment ensures that AI doesn't just serve a functional role but becomes a catalyst for achieving transformative outcomes.

Moreover, businesses should consider the scalability and adaptability of their AI solutions as fundamental benchmarks for success. The true potential of AI is realized when solutions can evolve and grow alongside business needs. This might mean adjusting AI capabilities to mirror changing market dynamics or expanding AI applications to new, unexplored areas of operations. Scalability ensures that the impact of AI remains positive and sustained, reflecting an organization's readiness to adapt rapidly in unforeseen circumstances.

It's also important to benchmark AI success against industry standards and regulatory compliance. Regularly comparing performance metrics with industry peers and considering standard best practices allows organizations to maintain a competitive edge. Compliance with regulatory standards not only averts legal repercussions but also propagates a culture of responsibility and integrity across the business spectrum.

Importantly, benchmarking AI-enabled success isn't just about quantitative metrics. Qualitative analysis—capturing stories of innovation, improvements in employee morale, and changes in customer experience—adds depth to any assessment. Perhaps a company's newfound capability to deliver personalized customer experiences or an enhanced company culture of innovation and learning are among the unseen benefits of AI that numbers alone can't depict. These intangible assets can be substantial drivers of business performance and should not be overlooked in the quest to benchmark success.

Another dynamic aspect of benchmarking AI-enabled success is the agility it brings to decision-making processes. AI can significantly accelerate decision-making by providing timely, data-driven insights. The capacity to make informed decisions rapidly can be a defining factor for businesses in competitive landscapes. By leveraging AI's ability to predict trends and behaviors, organizations can position themselves proactively rather than reactively, establishing a considerable market advantage.

Ultimately, successful benchmarking of AI initiatives requires a mindset shift toward an ongoing process of learning and adaptation. As AI technologies evolve and business environments shift, so too should benchmarks. Regular re-evaluation and updating of metrics ensure they remain relevant and aligned with the evolving landscape. Organizations that adopt a flexible, forward-thinking approach to benchmarking will be well-positioned to harness AI's full potential, driving sustained growth and competitive advantage.

In summary, benchmarking AI-enabled success is a multifaceted endeavor that requires a balance of quantitative measurements, qualitative insights, and strategic alignment. It demands vigilance in maintaining transparency and ensuring that AI systems operate ethically and efficiently. It also calls for an adaptability to change and a dedication to continual learning. By cultivating a comprehensive and responsive benchmarking strategy, business leaders will not only measure success effectively but also inspire confidence and create value for their organizations in the AI-driven economy.

Chapter 24:
Preparing for the Unknown

Stepping into the uncharted terrain of AI demands more than mere anticipation; it calls for a dynamic blend of foresight, resilience, and adaptability. As we journey deeper into this era of rapid technological transformation, the key to thriving lies in our ability to embrace uncertainty as a catalyst for innovation. Business leaders and tech enthusiasts alike must cultivate a mindset that not only expects the unexpected but is eager to harness it, transforming potential risks into opportunities. This chapter explores strategies for fortifying organizations against unforeseen challenges, emphasizing the importance of flexible frameworks, diverse skill sets, and a commitment to continuous learning. By fostering an environment that values agility and proactive governance, we empower ourselves to not just navigate but prosper amidst the unforeseen waves of AI advancements. Each development, while unpredictable, is a chance to redefine norms and expand our horizons, setting the stage for a future where preparedness and creative thinking become the twin pillars of success.

Anticipating Future Developments in AI

As we stand on the cusp of exponential technological advancements, anticipating future developments in AI becomes both an exciting and daunting task. In the past few decades, AI has rapidly evolved from a concept of science fiction to an integral part of our everyday lives and professional environments. This swift progression prompts a pressing question: What comes next? How do organizational leaders and tech enthusiasts prepare for the unknown, ensuring they're not just spectators but active shapers of future advancements?

First and foremost, the pace of AI research and development is accelerating. Innovations that once seemed years away are now at our doorstep. This demands an agile and proactive mindset among professionals and business leaders who seek to capitalize on AI's transformative potential. It's not about predicting the future with certainty but about creating adaptable strategies that embolden a company to pivot quickly in response to emerging technologies. This requires not just an awareness of technological trends but an openness to rethink traditional business models and paradigms continuously.

Moreover, the integration of AI with other emerging technologies such as quantum computing, the Internet of Things (IoT), and 5G connectivity suggests a horizon rich with potential advancements. Quantum computing, for instance, promises to supercharge AI capabilities, solving complex problems at unprecedented speeds. As these technologies merge, their collective impact could redefine industries beyond current imagination. The synergistic relationships among various tech domains could herald a renaissance of innovation, where AI acts as both a driver and a beneficiary of these developments.

One critical aspect of future AI development is democratization— a shift towards making advanced AI tools accessible to a broader audience. Low-code and no-code platforms are on the rise, enabling individuals without deep technical expertise to develop AI applications and solutions. This democratization has the potential to foster a more inclusive tech ecosystem, empowering a wider range of professionals to contribute to AI advancements. In this emerging landscape, organizations should cultivate internal cultures that encourage experimentation and learning. Emphasizing cross-disciplinary collaboration can spark innovations that resonate with diverse markets and communities.

However, with new opportunities come new challenges. As AI systems become more autonomous, ethical considerations will grow increasingly complex. Future developments in AI necessitate robust governance frameworks that address issues of accountability, transparency, and fairness. Businesses that prioritize aligning their AI strategies with ethical standards will likely gain public trust and remain resilient in times of scrutiny. Anticipating these challenges isn't just about legal compliance; it's about shaping AI technologies that reflect and elevate fundamental human values.

As AI continues to evolve, businesses might encounter unforeseen disruptions that challenge their established practices. Building resilience in the face of such uncertainty involves more than technology—it requires a shift in organizational culture towards one that embraces change and encourages forward-thinking leadership. Cultivating a mindset oriented towards continuous learning, innovation, and adaptability equips organizations to not only cope with but also thrive amid disruptive shifts.

The labor market is another critical frontier for AI's future impact. The technologies of tomorrow will very likely reevaluate which skills are most valued by employers and which roles can be automated or enhanced through AI. Emphasizing the improvement of soft skills such as creativity, emotional intelligence, and adaptability will become increasingly essential. Workers prepared to interact seamlessly with AI will find themselves in a position to harness these tools for heightened productivity and creativity.

Echoing these considerations is the imperative for international collaboration in AI advancements. As AI's global footprint expands, countries around the world will benefit from deeper partnerships that foster shared growth and innovation. This includes collaborative research efforts, harmonized regulatory approaches, and exchanges of best practices. A unified approach to developing AI technologies ensures a wide range of perspectives and talents are brought to the table, which ultimately benefits everyone involved.

In anticipating AI's future, one can imagine a landscape where AI-driven systems are ubiquitous, seamlessly integrating into our workflows and decision-making processes. However, the key lies not just in predicting individual technological breakthroughs but in understanding the cumulative effect these breakthroughs will have on society, businesses, and individuals. This understanding, coupled with prepared strategies and adaptable mindsets, allows for a future where the unknown does not incite fear but rather stimulates innovation and growth.

In summary, as we gaze into the future of AI, it's essential to balance optimism with realism. While AI promises to expand our capabilities and create tremendous opportunities, it also demands accountability and foresight. By embracing a proactive stance and fostering resilient and adaptable environments, professionals and organizations can navigate this exciting journey, positioning themselves at the forefront of transformative change. The future, while unpredictable, is writing itself through the steps we take today. Let's embrace the challenge and rise to meet it with informed, strategic action, ensuring that AI developments align with human prosperity.

Building Resilience in a Changing Landscape

In the ever-shifting world driven by AI advances, resilience has become not just a desirable trait but an essential one. As AI technologies continue to evolve at breakneck speed, organizations and individuals alike are faced with the challenge of staying ahead in an unpredictable environment. To maintain a competitive edge and ensure sustainability, resilience must be built into the very fabric of strategic planning and everyday operations.

Resilience doesn't just happen; it's a cultivated capability, honed over time with deliberate efforts and strategies. When it comes to AI, resilience requires a dual focus: thinking proactively about what's ahead and creating a responsive framework that adapts to unforeseen changes. An adaptive mindset encourages embracing change as an opportunity rather than fearing it as a threat. Essentially, it's about cultivating the ability to bounce back from disruption while seizing the new possibilities that such disruption unveils.

A key element in building resilience is the integration of robust data analytics. By leveraging advanced AI tools, companies can learn to anticipate market trends, identify potential disruptions before they occur, and adapt their strategies dynamically. Access to real-time data and the ability to predict outcomes not only help in decision-making but also in fostering a culture of agility and responsiveness within the organization. This predictive power allows businesses to stay one step ahead, ensuring they are prepared to weather any storm.

Equally important is the human aspect of resilience. While AI technology is a powerful enabler, it is still the human element that provides creativity, emotional intelligence, and ethical judgment — all crucial for long-term success. Thus, nurturing a workforce that is adaptable, open-minded, and ready to learn continuously is vital. This involves creating an environment that encourages experimentation, values diverse perspectives, and promotes shared learning experiences.

Organizations that focus on digital literacy programs can significantly enhance resilience. Providing employees with training opportunities to master AI-related skills ensures that they can better navigate the digital landscape. It's not just about understanding AI demystification; it's about integrating it into everyday roles to augment human potential and maintain the relevance of skill sets. This ongoing education help mitigate the fear of job obsolescence and replaces it with a sense of empowerment and possibility.

One of the most effective strategies for resilience building is establishing strong networks and partnerships. Collaboration is critical in an AI-driven landscape where innovation often emerges at the intersection of different industries and technological domains. By fostering a culture of collaboration, businesses can tap into external expertise and resources, thereby enhancing their adaptive capabilities. These partnerships create a value chain that is not only resilient but also continually evolving and growing stronger.

Furthermore, resilience in AI encompasses ethical considerations and cultural shifts. Ensuring fair and responsible AI implementation is crucial for maintaining trust with stakeholders. Businesses that embed ethical considerations in their AI strategies demonstrate a commitment to transparency and integrity, which solidifies their reputation even during challenging times. Having clear ethical guidelines helps navigate complex issues, from data privacy to algorithmic fairness, ensuring decisions are made with both foresight and accountability.

As the AI landscape evolves, leaders must recognize their role as visionaries and stewards of change. Effective leadership in times of rapid transformation involves not only a clear vision and strategic thinking but also the empathy and humility to inspire and motivate teams. Leaders must foster an organizational culture that not only embraces change but actively seeks it, creating an open dialogue about the challenges and opportunities AI presents.

In conclusion, building resilience in an AI-driven world is about preparing for the unknown while being flexible and innovative in approach. By combining strategic foresight with operational agility, organizations can ensure they're not just reacting to changes but are poised to capitalize on them. Ultimately, resilience becomes the competitive advantage that enables enduring success amid the shifting sands of technological advancement.

Chapter 25:
Collaborative AI: A New
Era of Innovation

The dawn of collaborative AI marks a transformative chapter in innovation, where technology and human ingenuity converge to create unparalleled possibilities. As artificial intelligence systems become more proficient at understanding and adapting to complex human needs, a symbiotic relationship emerges—one that enhances the capabilities of both man and machine. This evolution demands a reframing of our traditional roles, encouraging us to work alongside AI as partners rather than competitors. In this dynamic landscape, organizations that harness this synergy can unlock new levels of creativity and problem-solving, driving growth and competitiveness. By embracing collaborative AI, businesses are not just optimizing their operations but are paving the way for groundbreaking innovations that redefine industries. This new era challenges leaders to cultivate an environment where AI technologies are seamlessly integrated, fostering a culture that thrives on experimentation and forward-thinking strategies. Ultimately, the power of collaborative AI lies in its ability to amplify human potential, enabling us to achieve goals once thought unattainable and inspiring a future ripe with inventive solutions and transformative progress.

Case Studies of Successful AI Collaboration

In the era of Collaborative AI, the fusion between human ingenuity and artificial intelligence is no longer a distant vision but a present reality that's reshaping how we innovate and solve problems. Real-world instances of AI's seamless integration into diverse sectors reveal the profound possibilities when technology and human expertise unite. These stories are not just success stories; they're blueprints for others aiming to harness the transformative power of AI.

A standout example is the pharmaceutical industry, traditionally burdened by lengthy drug development cycles and high resource demands. Here, AI has emerged as a formidable ally, dramatically reducing the time required to bring new drugs to market. Take the partnership of a leading pharma company with an AI startup specializing in drug discovery. Their collaboration revolutionized the early phases of drug design, employing AI algorithms to predict molecular behavior more accurately and efficiently than traditional methods. This AI integration didn't just speed up the process; it also slashed costs, enabling the company to allocate resources more effectively and react to medical crises with unprecedented speed.

Meanwhile, in the financial sector, AI is redefining how organizations approach lending and risk management. A major bank collaborated with an AI firm to deploy a machine learning system that could analyze millions of data points in real time. This system was not only adept at predicting defaults with high accuracy but also assisted in personalizing customer experiences. By assessing risk more effectively and tailoring financial products to individual needs, the bank saw a significant boost in customer satisfaction and retention rates. This case demonstrates how AI can powerfully augment human decision-making, offering insights that are both deep and precise.

A third significant collaboration is found in the manufacturing industry, where AI's role in predictive maintenance is changing the game. One global manufacturing giant incorporated AI-driven analytics into their equipment maintenance schedule. By predicting equipment failures before they occurred, they reduced downtime and repair costs significantly. AI's predictive capabilities allowed the firm to optimize their operations beyond mere efficiency; it empowered them to innovate, reallocating saved resources towards research and development to enhance their competitive edge.

The creative industry is also experiencing a renaissance, thanks to AI collaboration. Consider a leading animation studio that integrated AI tools into their workflow. By leveraging AI for tasks like rendering and editing, the studio expedited production timelines and freed artists to focus on more creative aspects of their projects. AI didn't replace the artists; it enhanced their capabilities and expanded the studio's creative potential. This partnership illustrates AI's role as a collaborator rather than a competitor, enhancing human creativity rather than stifling it.

AI's impact on logistics and supply chain management has also been transformative. A prominent logistics firm adopted AI-enhanced routing algorithms that optimized delivery routes in real-time based on traffic data, weather conditions, and fleet logistics. The result was not only a drastic reduction in delivery times and operational costs but also a significant decrease in carbon emissions. This collaboration highlights how AI can contribute to more sustainable business practices, aligning operational efficiency with broader environmental goals.

In agriculture, AI is fostering a new wave of precision farming that challenges traditional cultivation methods. A collaboration between an agri-tech company and AI researchers led to the development of smart sensors and machine learning algorithms that monitor crop health, soil quality, and weather conditions. Farmers receive real-time data and actionable insights, enabling them to increase yields and reduce environmental impact. This AI-enabled approach empowers farmers with knowledge and tools that were previously unattainable, revolutionizing food production systems.

The healthcare industry, too, offers compelling narratives of AI collaboration. In one case, an AI and radiology department worked together to develop an algorithm that assists in early cancer detection. This tool analyzes radiology images with precision that rivals or even surpasses human experts. By flagging anomalies early, it extends the window for interventions and significantly improves patient outcomes. This model of collaboration doesn't just enhance diagnostic capabilities; it instills a new level of confidence in treatment protocols, giving healthcare professionals a potent ally in combating disease.

Lastly, the role of AI in education is gaining traction, with initiatives that personalize learning experiences for students. Adaptive learning platforms, created through partnerships between educational institutions and AI developers, tailor coursework to individual student needs, learning paces, and styles. Such personalization fosters a more engaging and effective learning environment, increasing the chances of student success and retention. These platforms exemplify how AI can assist educators in nurturing student potential, proving invaluable as educational landscapes evolve.

Across these diverse sectors, the central theme remains the same: successful AI collaboration hinges on leveraging AI's strengths while enhancing human expertise. These partnerships don't simply automate processes—they empower individuals and organizations to achieve what was previously unimaginable. As AI continues to evolve, these case studies provide a testament to its potential to drive significant innovations and improvements in countless industries.

In reflecting on these transformative collaborations, it's clear that AI, when used thoughtfully, can be a remarkable catalyst for change. These narratives serve as guiding stars for businesses and industries that are yet to embark on their AI journey, offering inspiration and tangible insights into the power of AI-driven collaboration. By embracing AI as a collaborative partner, organizations can unlock new levels of capability and vision, setting the stage for a future where human and machine creativity coalesce in unprecedented ways.

Lessons Learned from AI Integration

As the integration of artificial intelligence continues to redefine industries and reshape the global landscape, various lessons have emerged about what successful implementation looks like. From small-scale startups to large multinational corporations, those who have embraced AI have encountered insights that are shaping the future of work and innovation. These lessons are not merely technical but extend into organizational dynamics, cultural shifts, and even ethical considerations.

The first critical lesson is that AI integration requires a deep understanding of both the technical capabilities and the business goals it aims to serve. It's not enough to adopt AI technologies for their own sake. Companies need to align AI applications with their strategic objectives to drive true value. This alignment often demands a shift in mindset—leaders must cultivate a vision that sees AI as an enabler of growth rather than a mere tool for solving existing problems.

Collaboration across departments is another indispensable insight derived from AI integration. Successful initiatives are characterized by a synergy between technical teams and business units. Data scientists, for instance, should work closely with marketers, product developers, and customer service teams to ensure that AI-driven insights are actionable and aligned with broader company objectives. This cross-functional collaboration transforms disparate data into actionable insights, fueling informed decision-making and innovation.

Organizations have also learned that integrating AI is not a one-time event but a continuous journey. Maintaining an adaptive mindset is crucial. The technology is ever-evolving, and so are business environments. Companies must keep abreast of the latest developments in AI research and application to stay competitive. Investing in continuous learning and upskilling for employees is integral to this process. It ensures that the workforce remains agile and capable of leveraging new AI capabilities effectively.

Another lesson involves the importance of managing data effectively. AI thrives on data, and the quality of input invariably affects the quality of output. Companies have realized the necessity of having robust data governance frameworks in place. This includes not just collecting and storing data but also ensuring its accuracy, relevance, and compliance with privacy regulations. Reliable data can be a formidable competitive advantage, facilitating accurate predictions and more personalized customer experiences.

Ethical considerations and responsible AI usage have emerged as critical learning points as well. Integrating AI responsibly means acknowledging and addressing potential biases inherent in algorithms. Companies must develop protocols for auditing AI systems to mitigate any unintended consequences, such as discrimination or privacy invasion. This responsibility extends to ensuring transparency in AI operations, fostering trust among customers and stakeholders alike.

The integration of AI into business operations has also underscored the importance of fostering a culture of innovation. As AI takes on routine tasks, human creativity, and strategic thinking become even more valuable. Companies should encourage an atmosphere where experimentation is welcomed, failures are seen as learning opportunities, and innovative ideas can surface and be tested rapidly.

Importantly, businesses have learned that a comprehensive strategy must involve not only advanced technology but also people-centric approaches. AI should enhance how humans work rather than replace them. When employees understand that AI is a tool to augment their capabilities, they are more likely to embrace it. This approach can lead to increased productivity, job satisfaction, and the unlocking of human potential.

On a strategic level, the lesson is clear that leaders should take a proactive stance in shaping the AI narrative within their organizations. This involves clear communication about AI's role and potential benefits, setting realistic expectations, and maintaining transparency in AI-led changes. Leaders must also be prepared to navigate the complexities and uncertainties that come with the adoption of AI technologies, managing any resistances smoothly and effectively.

Moreover, successful AI integration underscores the need for flexible and agile organizational structures. Traditional siloed departments often hinder the fluid exchange of ideas and rapid implementation of AI initiatives. Embracing more dynamic, team-oriented structures can enable quicker adaptation to changing technological landscapes and more effective collaboration across various operational domains.

The process also highlights the importance of partnerships and collaborative efforts beyond an organization's walls. Engaging with AI consortiums, academic institutions, and even competitors in some instances, can open avenues for accessing cutting-edge research, exchanging knowledge, and co-creating advanced solutions that a single entity could not achieve alone. This external engagement can be a cornerstone for fostering innovation and ensuring sustainable growth in an AI-driven marketplace.

Another valuable lesson is the necessity of evolving leadership to meet the demands of AI transformation. Leaders need to be visionaries, capable of understanding the long-term implications of AI and steering the company in a direction that leverages technological advancements while upholding human value and ethics. Those at the helm must be educated about AI, its capabilities, and its limitations, empowering them to make informed decisions that balance technological potential with human considerations.

Ultimately, the confluence of these lessons leads to a holistic understanding that AI integration is not only about technology; it's about crafting an ecosystem that harmonizes machines and humans for mutual growth. This approach calls for new forms of leadership, continuous learning, and a willingness to adapt. Businesses that internalize these lessons are not only poised to excel in today's competitive landscape but are also set to lead in the future, driving innovations that benefit society as a whole.

In conclusion, AI integration presents companies with opportunities and challenges in equal measure. Navigating this complex terrain demands openness to learning, adaptation, and a committed focus on aligning AI capabilities with human and organizational goals. As we continue to learn and grow, these lessons form a crucial roadmap, guiding us toward a collaborative and innovative future where AI and humans coalesce for the greater good.

Conclusion

As we stand on the precipice of a new age defined by artificial intelligence, it's vital to embrace both the opportunities and the challenges that come with it. The landscape of work is rapidly changing, and those who adapt with foresight and agility will undoubtedly thrive. This book has journeyed through the intricacies of AI's impact on traditional work environments, offering strategies to prepare for an AI-driven future.

AI is reshaping industries, roles, and expectations at an unprecedented rate. Its potential to transform business practices and enhance productivity is vast and ever-expanding. However, this transformation isn't purely technological. It's as much about the human element—how we collaborate with machines and how we redefine what it means to succeed in our professional lives.

For business leaders and professionals, the call to action is clear: cultivate a mindset of resilience and adaptability. Lifelong learning isn't merely a recommendation; it's a necessity in this evolving landscape. Upskilling and reskilling will help individuals stay relevant and valuable as AI continues to alter job roles and industry demands.

Ethical considerations remain at the forefront of AI deployment. Responsible AI usage ensures that while we harness its capabilities, we also safeguard human rights and prioritize human-centric values. Addressing issues like bias, transparency, and accountability is not optional; it is essential for sustainable development and trust in AI systems.

Organizations must foster cultures that welcome innovation and experimentation. Strategies should be developed with a keen awareness of potential disruptions while embracing the adaptability and ingenuity AI offers. By integrating AI thoughtfully, businesses can drive growth, enhance customer experiences, and leverage data to make informed decisions.

Leaders of tomorrow will need to possess not just technological acumen but also the vision to lead teams through change and uncertainty. They will play a crucial role in creating environments where employees feel empowered to learn and innovate alongside AI. This partnership between human creativity and AI efficiency will be key to unlocking new potential.

Globally, AI's impact on the economy and international collaboration opens new avenues for growth and development. Countries and companies alike need to align their AI strategies with global standards and cooperate on ethical norms and regulations to ensure a balanced and fair future.

In conclusion, the AI era presents a world of possibilities balanced by responsibilities. By focusing on human-centric approaches and embracing change with open arms, we can create a future where AI acts as a collaborator rather than a competitor. It's a time for courage, curiosity, and collaboration—a time to redefine what it means to work and to succeed in a world where artificial intelligence is an integral partner.

Appendix A:
Resources for Further Learning

In an age where artificial intelligence is reshaping every facet of the workplace, staying informed about the latest developments, technologies, and best practices is crucial for maintaining a competitive edge. We've compiled a selection of resources that can empower you to delve deeper into AI's transformative impact and help you adapt to the changing landscape. The following resources span books, online courses, podcasts, and industry reports to provide comprehensive learning opportunities for professionals, business leaders, and tech enthusiasts alike.

Books

The AI Advantage: How to Put the Artificial Intelligence Revolution to Work by Thomas H. Davenport - This book provides practical advice on how organizations can leverage AI to enhance business processes and maintain competitiveness.

Prediction Machines: The Simple Economics of Artificial Intelligence by Ajay Agrawal, Joshua Gans, and Avi Goldfarb - A must-read for understanding the economic impact of AI and how prediction technologies can be harnessed in business decisions.

Superintelligence: Paths, Dangers, Strategies by Nick Bostrom - Explore the future of AI and its potential implications for humanity with this thought-provoking examination of superintelligent machines.

Online Courses

Coursera's *AI For Everyone* - Taught by Andrew Ng, this course offers a non-technical overview of AI, explaining its capabilities and applications in various sectors.

edX's *Artificial Intelligence MicroMasters Program* by Columbia University - This program covers the essential principles of AI, including robotics, machine learning, and computer vision.

Udacity's *AI and Robotics Nanodegree* - Gain a deeper understanding of AI's role in robotics with hands-on projects and real-world applications.

Podcasts

AI Alignment Podcast - Dive into discussions about the alignment of AI systems with human values, featuring leading thinkers in the field.

Exponential View by Azeem Azhar - Each episode covers the implications of cutting-edge technologies, including AI, on business and society.

Talking Machines - A podcast dedicated to the latest in machine learning and AI, featuring interviews with top researchers and insights into current trends.

Industry Reports

McKinsey Global Institute's Artificial Intelligence: The Next Digital Frontier? - This report investigates the opportunities and challenges of AI adoption across industries.

PwC's AI Predictions Series - An annual series that provides insights into the future impact of AI innovations on global industries.

The AI Index Report - A comprehensive annual report that tracks, collates, distills, and visualizes data relating to AI to provide a clearer picture of recent trends and technical advancements.

With these resources, you can explore the dynamic world of AI, gain deeper insights into its applications, and stay ahead of the curve. Learning and adapting continuously will enable you to leverage AI effectively in your professional pursuits, driving both personal and organizational growth in an AI-driven future.